Political Science on the Internet 1998–1999:

A Prentice Hall Guide

Political Science on the Internet 1998–1999:
A Prentice Hall Guide

Andrew T. Stull

Edited by
V.J. Benokraitis
Shepherd College

Adapted for Political Science by
James A. Puetz
North Harris College

Prentice Hall, *Upper Saddle River, NJ 07458*

Copyright © 1999 by Prentice-Hall, Inc.
Simon & Schuster/A Viacom Company
Upper Saddle River, New Jersey 07458

Printed in the United States of America

All rights reserved. No part of this book may be reproduced or transmitted in any form or by any means, electronic or mechanical, including photocopying, recording, or any information storage and retrieval system, without permission in writing from the publisher.

10 9 8 7 6 5 4 3 2 1

ISBN 0-13-978768-2

TRADEMARK INFORMATION:
America Online is a registered trademark of Quantum Computer Services Incorporated;
CompuServe is a trademark of CompuServe, Incorporated;
Windows is a trademark of Microsoft Corporation;
Mosaic is a trademark of the National Center for Supercomputing Applications;
Navigator is a registered trademark of Netscape Communications Corporation;
Java is a registered trademark of Sun Microsystems.

The authors and publisher of this manual have used their best efforts in preparing this book. The authors and publisher make no warranty of any kind, expressed or implied, with regard to these programs or the documentation contained in this book. The author and publisher shall not be liable in any event for incidental or consequential damages in connection with, or arising out of, the furnishing, performance, or use of the programs described in this book.

Contents

Preface Change! vii

Introduction O' Brave New World: Brief Internet History ix

Chapter 1 What Makes It Tick? The Basics 1

    1.1 Springs, wheels, and dials—Connecting 1
    1.2 Putting the pieces together—Organizing 6
    Activity: *The Starting Line* 9

Chapter 2 Hitting the Road: Mapping the Net 10

    2.1 Cruising the Net—Browsing 10
    2.2 Landmarks—Navigating 14
    2.3 Asking for directions—Searching 18
    Activity: *The Great Cybertrip* 22

Chapter 3 Traveling in Style: As You Like It 23

    3.1 Coffee, tea, or milk?—Customizing 23
    3.2 Wish you were here—Communicating 28
    3.3 The fun is in the going—Extending 36
    Activity: *A Talkabout Tour* 39

Chapter 4 Back to the Future: Advanced Techniques 40

    4.1 There's no place like home—Designing 40

    4.2   Opening your own shop—Serving   51
           Activity: *Show that You've Arrived*   54

Appendix I   Stepping Out: Student Homepage Template   55

Appendix II   Internet Resources for Political Science   58

Appendix III   Documenting Your Electronic Sources   71

Glossary   Fasten Your Seatbelts: Jargon to Go   76

Preface
Change!

The artist picks up the message of cultural and technological challenge decades before its transforming impact occurs.*

Change! The original edition of this manual gasped its first breath at 7:22 p.m. on July 23, 1995. Since then, a great deal about the World Wide Web and the world at large has changed. Our world is louder, faster, and more complex than the one experienced by earlier generations. In terms of information transfer, we might be described as a techno-generation; our parents, as a paper-generation. The World Wide Web has changed as well, and it will probably continue to do so; our online future is likely to be chaotic but exciting. Prepare to revel in the difference that tomorrow will bring.

Reading this manual won't teach you all there is to know about the World Wide Web, but it will help you to teach yourself. In the future you will need to find information for yourself rather than relying solely on others, who may bear outdated knowledge. If you are successful, your skills in "cruising" the Internet will allow you to deal with ongoing change. By the end of this manual, you should be comfortable and resourceful in navigating the complexity of the Internet, from its back eddies to its thriving thoroughfares.

This manual has four chapters. In the Introduction, *O' Brave New World*, we will describe the origin of and the innovations behind the Internet. In Chapter 1, *What Makes It Tick?*, we will explain the use of a Web browser and describe how you can connect to the Internet. The boxed and end-of-chapter exercises will give you practice in using your browser as well as introduce you to some of the wonderful places on the Internet.

In Chapter Two, *Hitting the Road*, you'll learn more about how to use your browser in order to cruise the endless byways of the Internet. Also, you

---

*After each major heading, you'll see a quote from *Understanding Media, The Extensions of Man* (MIT Press, Cambridge, MA, 1964) by Marshall McLuhan. See also "McLuhan Meets the Net," by Larry Press, Communications of the ACM, July 1995.

will be introduced to resources and strategies for information searching. The boxed and end-of-chapter exercises will reinforce your navigational skills and give you practice in searching for some of the great Political Science sites on the Internet. These resources, along with related newsgroups, appear in Appendix II.

In Chapter Three, *Traveling in Style*, you will learn how to customize your Web browser to make it more responsive to your needs. You will find yourself changing from an observer into an enthusiastic Internet participant. The boxed and end-of-chapter exercises will help you contact others on the Internet.

In Chapter Four, *Back to the Future*, you will move into the fast lane of Web publishing. We'll discuss the ins and outs of Web design, HTML editing software, and Web server development.

In addition to the Internet resources listed in Appendix II, a student homepage template is provided in Appendix I. Finally, a glossary defines the buzzwords.

Introduction
O' Brave New World
Brief Internet History

As electrically constructed, the globe is no more than a village.

This thing that we now call the Internet has been evolving ever since it was first developed over twenty-five years ago. Many people have compared the Internet to a living creature because of the way it grows and changes. You may find its history quite interesting.

In the late 1950s and early 1960s, scientists and engineers realized the importance of sharing information and communicating through their computers. Many different groups attempted to develop computer network languages that would enable computers to exchange information with one another. But unfortunately, all of these computer systems used different languages—people on different systems still had difficulty communicating with one another. It was like the Tower of Babel all over again.

The Internet was born as the solution to this problem. The U.S. government paid for the development of a common network language, called a protocol, which was eventually shared freely. Over time, many formerly isolated networks from all over the world adopted this language. Thus, the best description of the Internet is that it is not a network, but a network of networks. However, the Internet is independent of governments and regulation—there is no central Internet agency. Change is spurred by the common needs of the people that use the Internet.

Admittedly, this type of network system isn't the most graceful—but it works. If you saw a diagram of this great big computer network, you might find it resembles a spider's web. On this web, information can travel between any two points along any one of many possible paths.

Originally, the chief purpose of the Internet was to provide a distribution system for scientific exchange and research. Gradually, however, the

Internet also became a digital post office, enabling people to send mail and transfer computer files electronically. Although the Internet is still used extensively by scientists, the commercial sector is currently the most powerful force behind its growth.

As technology changed, the speed with which information could be transferred and the way we viewed information changed. In 1991, an important new user interface was developed at the University of Minnesota: the *Gopher*. *Gopher* is a visually-oriented search tool for the Internet that allows users to locate information found on other computers. Because of *Gopher*, and other, more sophisticated *graphical user interfaces* developed since 1991, it is now possible to search through vast stores of information on computers all over the world. Once the desired information is found, it can be easily downloaded to the user's computer. Amazing if you think about it! You could be on your computer in Shepherdstown, West Virginia, and view information from London, Mexico City, or Tokyo without even realizing it. Wham! And no airline tickets!

In 1992, researchers in Switzerland helped to create a new format for information exchange that led to the explosive growth of the World Wide Web (WWW). Information on the Web is posted as a "page" that may contain text, images, sounds, and even movies. The organization of a page is much like any printed page in a book. However, Web pages make use of *hypermedia*. Hypermedia involves the use of words and images as links, or connecting points, between different texts, images, sounds, or movies on other computers throughout the world. *Hypertext* Web pages contain links only to other text documents.

However, the introduction of the Web created a dilemma: It was a great place to go, but there was no easy way to get there. We still lacked a convenient software program that would allow users to access the Web easily. In 1993, a program called *Mosaic* was developed by the National Center for Supercomputing Applications (NCSA). It allowed the user to browse Web pages as well as use other Internet resources such as electronic mail (e-mail).

In 1991, around 700,000 people were using the Internet. After the introduction of *Mosaic*, users increased to around 1.7 million. Upon the release of Netscape *Navigator*, users were estimated at 3.2 million. Since then, the growth hasn't slowed much—various estimates suggest that the number of people who have access to the Internet ranges from 20 million to 100 million.

Just listen to the popular media. When was the last time you saw a television program, heard a radio commercial, or read a magazine without encountering something about the Internet? Today, you have access to animation, video clips, audio files, and even virtual reality worlds. Imagine all the new ways we will be able to view tomorrow's digital world.

For those of you who already have some Web experience, here are a few Web addresses discussing the history and growth of the Internet. Simply type the address into your Web browser exactly as it appears below. If you are just beginning to learn about the Internet, you might want to visit these sites after you learn more about Web browsers and Internet addresses in Chapter 2.

BBN Timeline
BBN includes an Internet history timeline. It places the important Internet events in context with other historical events and throws in plenty of social commentary to give you perspective.
Address: http://www.bbn.com/timeline

Hobbes' Internet Timeline
Hobbes' site offers a great deal about the Internet, the people who use it, and online culture.
Address: http://info.isoc.org/guest/zakon/Internet/History/HIT.html

Netizens: On the History and Impact of Usenet and the Internet
This is a comprehensive collection of essays about the history, nature, and impact of the Internet.
Address: http://www.columbia.edu/~hauben/netbook/

Political Science on the Internet 1998–1999:

A Prentice Hall Guide

Chapter 1
What Makes It Tick?
The Basics

*An Indian is the servomechanism of his canoe,
as the cowboy of his horse or the executive of his clock.*

Many of you reading this manual have a lot of experience with computers, while others have little or none. In the first section of this chapter, we will briefly describe the basic computer setup you'll need, how to use a modem, and choose an Internet Service Provider (ISP). Many of you may have computers on your campus that are set up to allow Internet access. In case you don't, we'll list the minimum in terms of systems, connections, and services that you'll need for the Internet.

In the second section of this chapter, we will explain some of the idiosyncrasies of the Internet and describe the general features of most Internet browser software. A popular Web browser, Netscape *Navigator*, is used to illustrate discussions. Another popular browser is Microsoft *Internet Explorer*. Both are *free* to students. We don't advocate any particular browser; you will probably want to try various browsers and make up your own mind. Although our illustrations focus on *Navigator*, fear not; browsers share many of the same features. Once you've learned the basic techniques, it's easy to switch back and forth.

Section 1.1
Springs, wheels, and dials—Connecting

What is the difference between a Rolex and a Timex? Without much consideration, the main difference is the price. But if we consider how well each of these watches meets our basic need for being on time, the two watches are very similar. The same goes for computers and networks. The simple no-frills components will save you money; the high-gloss gear will transform your cash into dash and make your Internet browsing only a little more enjoyable.

To get started, you'll need a *computer*, a *modem*, an *Internet connection*, and *browser software*. The descriptions that follow will help you understand each component and its function to access the Internet.

The Computer

Be careful how you approach this issue if you ask someone for advice on which computer to buy. Many people have strong opinions about the differences between Macintosh and PC-compatible systems. The best advice that we can give to you is to test them both at a computer store. Choose the one that you can pay for and are most comfortable using.

These are the *minimum* system configurations that you'll need:

Macintosh
- 68030
- MacOS 7.0
- 256 color monitor
- 16 MB of RAM
- 8 MB of free disk space for browser software

PC-Compatible
- Intel 486
- Windows 3.1
- VGA monitor
- 16 MB of RAM
- 8 MB of free disk space for browser software

If you are purchasing a new computer, the minimum may not be readily available and therefore is not recommended. Stepping up to a PowerMac (with MacOS 7.6 or higher) or a Pentium-based PC (with Windows 9x) would be more desirable.

A new innovation is the Network Computer, or NC. An NC is a computer without all of the software that you expect in an ordinary computer: word processing, drawing, graphing, and number crunching. Because these features may be helpful to you, you should consider the purchase of an NC carefully. An NC (a box that sits on top of your TV) will allow you to connect your television directly to the Internet. *Web*TV is currently the most popular, but we suspect that you'll see many different brands in the future. The advantage of such products is that they are much cheaper than an ordinary (but more capable) computer. Also, you don't have to be a computer whiz to use them.

The Modem

You probably want to know why you need a modem if you already have a computer. A modem is a device that MOdulates and DEModulates—that is, it translates a computer signal into a telephone signal, and vice versa. Although computers and telephones were set up to speak different "languages," you can use a modem to translate between your computer and another computer across your telephone line. Modems come in different "sizes," so don't just go out and buy the cheapest one on sale. Definitely don't buy one from a garage sale unless you really know what you're doing. Because modem technology changes so quickly, older equipment may be useful only as a doorstop. The number one thing that you need to know about a modem is its speed of transmission. Modem speeds are referred to in units called baud (a bit is a basic unit of digital information and a baud is the speed of transmitting 1 bit in 1 second). At one time a modem speed of 2600 baud was considered adequate. However, the minimum speed requirements have been steadily increasing as users demand more information at faster rates. You should purchase a modem with a speed of at least 28,800 baud (28.8K baud). With a 28.8K baud modem you can expect that it will take a few seconds to transfer a typical Web page. However, keep in mind that manufacturers will continue to introduce newer and faster modems as pages become more complex and as users demand faster speeds. For example, two competing products using proprietary standards are offering 56K baud modems. Until a uniform standard is established, itís probably wiser to wait before buying these faster modems. (If the site hasn't changed by the time you read this, connect to **http://www.miningcom.com** for the latest on buying of new modem. The site is useful on its own, though.)

You also need to make sure that your modem will work with your computer's operating system. Generally, this isn't a big deal, as all modems are basically the same and top manufacturers produce software for all of the major operating systems. Just remember to read the box to make sure it contains the software you need. Included with the software is an installation manual and a phone number to a help desk. If you run into trouble, don't hesitate to try both. As for which brand of modem to purchase, buy what you can afford. Your Internet Service Provider or your campus computer administrator may recommend a particular brand of modem. Take this suggestion seriously. The technicians within your ISP or campus are likely to be familiar with the recommended modem and will be able to help you if problems arise.

The word modem may also refer to a device that allows you to connect your computer or television to a service line. By the time this guide is published, you will undoubtedly hear of things called ISDN modems and cable modems. An ISDN modem is a classic misnomer because the ISDN signal is already understood by computers and isn't modulated and doesn't need to be demodulated. The cable modem refers to a box that connects between your cable TV line (not your telephone line) and your computer or television.

The Internet Connection

Your campus may already be using the Internet as a teaching and learning tool. If not, there are many resources to help you set up a connection from home.

Some campuses, although lacking a walk-in lab, have made arrangements for students to dial into the campus computer system and connect to the Internet with a modem. If this is the case, search out the campus computer guru and ask for help.

Another option is to subscribe to a company such as *America Online*, *CompuServe*, *Microsoft Network*, or one of the many independent Mom and Pop companies currently offering monthly access to the Internet. It is a buyer's market and you should shop around. Test drive everything before you buy. This will save you a great deal of frustration. Here are a few things to consider when choosing an Internet Service Provider:

Does the ISP have a local number for your area? You need to call the provider each time you access the Internet. Paying a toll call every time you do so will become costly if you use the Internet regularly.

Can their system handle a large number of simultaneous connections? Ask them how many users they can handle at one time and how many subscribers they have. Although they may have a reasonable price and a local number, it doesn't mean much if you can't get on to use it. If after you subscribe you find that you are never able to connect or that the only available access is late at night or early in the morning, find a new ISP.

Do they offer SLIP/PPP connections? This is the type of connection that you'll need if you want to use a graphical browser like Navigator or Internet Explorer. Some ISPs only offer shell accounts. Shell accounts require you to type in each command as you would with a command-line interface such as provided in DOS. It is somewhat like driving a horse and buggy when everyone else has an automobile.

Do they have a reasonable monthly subscription fee? Cheapest is not always best. The added features and the staffing support are important points to consider when choosing a service. Some Internet Service Providers offer you unlimited monthly connect time for a flat fee and others charge for a specific number of hours per month (with hourly rates thereafter). Estimate your expected usage and purchase accordingly. Ask if there is a fee to upgrade your service if you find that you need more time. If you have a roommate, consider upgrading the service and splitting the cost. This may save you money.

Does your ISP include the Internet browser software in the price? You'll find that not all do. Most ISPs have an agreement with either Netscape or Microsoft to bundle their browser software. The provided software may also be partially configured to work on the ISP's system. Moreover, the technicians will be better able to help you with a problem.

Is the ISP a regional or local company? This may not be important to everyone, but some of you may go home during holidays and vacations. If the ISP covers a wider area, then you can still check your e-mail and cruise the Net when you are away from school.

Do they have a help line in case you need technical assistance to set up your connection? Call the help line before you subscribe and make sure you get a real person. Although you may be asked to leave your name and number, you should expect to get a return call within 24 hours. If they don't return your call within this period, then the service is probably understaffed or poorly managed.

Does the ISP offer both newsgroup and e-mail access in addition to a connection to the *Web*? This is usually standard but there are always exceptions.

Does it cost you extra for additional e-mail addresses? If you have a roommate, then you may find that it is more affordable to split the cost of a subscription and pay for an additional e-mail account.

Will your ISP add newsgroups at your request? Most ISPs subscribe to a small fraction of the available newsgroups and you may find that they don't include some of the basic, academic groups that your instructors may recommend. It shouldn't cost anything for the ISP to add these groups to their list.

Does the ISP offer you space for your own Web page? Often, one of the features offered in the basic package is the option of posting your own homepage. A limited amount of memory will be provided by the ISP.

The most important thing to remember when using an ISP is to expect courteous and prompt service. If you don't like what you are paying for, then cancel and go somewhere else. There are plenty of competitors willing to offer you better service.

The Browser Software

A descriptive name for software such as *Navigator* or *Internet Explorer* is *browser* software, because that is what most people do with it. It is used to browse or wander, sometimes aimlessly, through the Internet.

Many Web browsers are on the market today, and new ones frequently enter the race to capture your dollar.

All browsers have advantages and disadvantages. You should evaluate several and choose the one that is most comfortable for you. (However, when choosing a browser, remember that seeing over the dashboard is all that is really important. Don't get wrapped up in features that you'll never use.) *Navigator, Internet Explorer*, and many of the other browsers are free for student use! Don't be afraid to look at several. At the end of the chapter you will find several Web addresses that offer such software. Of course, if you purchase the browser at the store, you also get a user's manual, which you don't get with the free, educational copy.

If you have all of these basic elements and they've been put together correctly, you should be ready to surf. (See the activity at the end of this chapter, *The Starting Line*.) The rest of this manual is devoted to guiding you through some of the wonderful places that will allow you to enjoy the depth and scope of Political Science.

Section 1.2
Putting the pieces together—Organizing

The software that you'll use to access the Net is commonly called a *Client* or a Web *browser*. It functions according to an information exchange model called the *Client-Server model* (Figure 1.1). In this way, a *client* (your Web browser software) communicates with a server (a computer with Web server software) on the Internet to exchange information. When referring to the Web, the information that your browser receives from the server is called a page.

What really appears on these Web pages? The best way to find out is to see for yourself. Sit down in front of a computer, start your browser software, and connect to the Internet. Your browser is probably already set to start at a specific page. This start page is often referred to as a *homepage*. Web pages usually include both text and images. Some also use sounds and videos. The use of different information types is called multimedia. A basic rule of the road is that anything that can be saved or recorded onto a computer can be distributed on the Internet through a Web page.

When you choose a page it will be sent to your computer. After the requested information has been sent by the server, your computer will display it for you. However, sometimes the Internet is not as responsive as you'd like. (Why

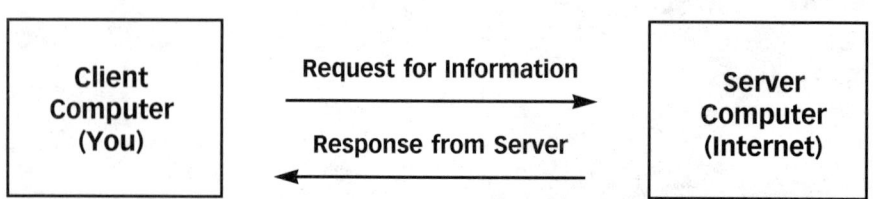

Figure 1.1. The client requests information from the server. The requested information is displayed on the client computer.

do you think some people refer to the World Wide Web as the World Wide Wait?) A few analogies and real-world considerations may help you see why this is so.

Patchwork Quilts

The patchwork quilt you might use during cold nights is one analogy. The quilt may have been crafted by your grandmother. Or in another time, a community of women (not all with equal sewing talent) may have met to produce a single quilt from a collection of patches differing in color, shape, and pattern. Due to the complexity, age, use, care, and variations in craftsmanship, quilts eventually become threadbare and require mending. The Internet is just like your favorite quilt in this respect.

Spider Webs

As we mentioned in the introduction, the Internet can be thought of as a big spider web. If you're the spider and you're trying to get to a fly stuck in the web, you usually have more than one path to get there. Some paths are more direct than others, but there are choices. Like a spider web, sometimes a small section of the Internet drops out of the "Web" and traffic has to be rerouted. This obviously causes increased traffic on the remaining strands, which in turn increases your waiting time.

Far Away Places

Remember that the Internet mimics the real world. Distance is a factor in determining how long it takes to access a Web page. Generally, loading a page from a machine across town is much faster than loading a page from across the nation or across the world.

Time Zones and Lunch

The world works on different time zones and the Internet does too. And what about lunch? Most people in the Western world take lunch around noon, and many of them check their e-mail or browse the Web as well. You can usually expect Internet traffic to be slow during that time. Let's now consider the distance factor. There is a three-hour time difference between the East and West coasts of North America, so the lunch rush lasts about four hours. Your location will determine if you are on the lead, middle, or tail end of the rush. Plan accordingly.

Parking Lots

Surfing the Web can be like shopping during the holidays. You either arrive early or park a few miles away. Here's the connection: A transaction occurs between your computer and another when you load a Web page for viewing. You require a document (a Web page) from somewhere on the Internet (a server). Obviously, a slow connection to the Internet on the client side may cause delays. But consider what is happening on the server end of the transaction. Small, slow servers will take longer to serve Web pages than large, fast servers. Now think about the holiday rush: Although there is normally adequate parking, a holiday sale and a limited number of parking spaces can add hours to your shopping. It should not be difficult to see how large, fast servers can be rapidly overloaded if they are hosting a really interesting Web site.

When Microsoft released an updated version of Internet Explorer, over twenty state-of-the-art machines went down because of excessive demand. Basically, Microsoft's parking lot wasn't big enough for the shopping rush.

By this time, you probably understand enough about each of the basic components of an Internet to try it out. Even if you're feeling unsure, don't worry. You don't need to know everything there is to know about each component. And you can always learn more from the user's guides provided by the manufacturers. Just take it one step at a time and you'll piece everything together.

Activity:
The Starting Line

There's no better time than now to get started. And you really don't need a destination to have fun. This activity is intended to help you get ready to cruise or surf the Internet. Even if you don't have a computer to access the Internet, use a friend's computer or one on campus to view this material.

The Browser
You should have a computer and a modem. Use the following Internet addresses to research the right browser for you.

> **Netscape**
> http://www.netscape.com
> **Microsoft**
> http://www.microsoft.com
> **Browserwatch**
> http://browserwatch.internet.com

The Internet Service Provider
With your computer, modem, *and* browser, you're only one step away. Use the following Internet addresses to research the right ISP for you.

> **Choosing the Internet Service Provider (Netscape)**
> http://home.netscape.com/assist/isp_select/index.html
> **Internet Access Provider Guide**
> http://www.liii.com/~dhjordan/students/docs/welcome.htm
> **Choosing An Internet Provider**
> http://tcp.ca/Dec95/Commtalk_ToC.html
> **Internet Service Providers by Area Code**
> http://thelist.internet.com

Research
It's always nice to have an independent opinion; therefore, read what the critics have to say. The following Internet addresses are for two of the largest publishers of computer-related magazines. Between them, they print nearly 50 different popular periodicals about computers and the Internet. Search their databases for articles that will help you make Internet decisions. You can read the articles online.

> **CMP Media** (Publisher of *Windows Magazine* and others)
> http://www.techweb.com/info/publications/publications.html
> **Ziff Davis** (Publisher of *PC Magazine*, *MacWeek*, and others)
> http://www5.zdnet.com/findit/search.html

Chapter 2
Hitting the Road
Mapping the Net

> *Under electronic technology the entire business of man becomes learning and knowing.*

By now, you should be prepared to see the world, or at least the World Wide Web. In this chapter, you'll develop a better understanding of the browser as a tool for navigating the Internet. The first section discusses basic navigation techniques; the second describes how to read Internet addresses; and the third introduces you to some of the information tools available on the Internet for finding your way around.

Section 2.1
Cruising the Net—Browsing

Even though the Internet is vast, finding your way around is no harder then finding your way to a friend's house. Information on the Internet has an address just as your friends do. Most browsers allow you to type in an address and thereby access information, or "go to" a particular document.

Let's take a look at how to enter an address using the Web browser Netscape *Navigator*, shown in Figure 2.1. Start by finding the text entry box, which is located to the right of the words *GoTo*. (Sometimes the word *Location* is used instead.) If you have *Navigator*, type in the address and press the return button on your keyboard.

Now take a look at the row of boxes directly above the text box. Each one contains an icon; together, they are known as the *tool bar*. Clicking on an individual box causes the computer to execute the command in the box.

How do each of these commands help you navigate the Internet? Let's return to our analogy. Suppose you go to a friend's new home for a party but

Figure 2.1. The tool bar for Netscape *Navigator* offers basic navigation features such as *Back*, *Forward*, and *Home*. You will find everything you'll need to navigate around the Internet.

forget the house-warming present. What do you do? Drive home, of course. A Web browser will let you do something similar. In Figure 2.1, find the button labeled *Back*—it's at the far left. By clicking on this button you can return to the Web page you just visited. If you have gone to many Web pages, you can use it repeatedly to make your way back to your starting point.

> Here is the address of a site you might want to visit. When you type it into your browser, you will arrive at *NewsLink*, which is published by Simon and Schuster. It is not free but it is very reasonable and very good.
>
> **http://www.ssnewslink.com**
>
> *NewsLink* is a subscription service that you can use to get news delivered. Among others, the Associated Press and *US News and World Report* provide free news services. You can reach them at the following addresses:
>
> **http://wire.ap.org**
>
> **http://www.usnews.com/usnews/home/htm**

Now find the *Home* button. By selecting this button, you will immediately return to the homepage configured for your browser. When you first begin using your browser, it will be set to a page determined by the company that created it. Later on, you'll learn how to make any page you wish into a homepage and even to create your own. But for now, remember that you can always go home.

Two other buttons common to most browsers are *Stop* and *Reload*. *Stop* is pretty easy to understand but *Reload* needs just a bit more explanation. As you explore more of the Internet, you'll realize that complete pages don't show up in your browser window instantly. Instead, different types of elements (pictures, icons, text, animations, etc.) appear over time as they are moved from the server to your browser. Occasionally, you'll notice that a page loads without some of these elements. This is often caused by an error in the transmission. Use the *Reload* button to request a new copy of the page.

You don't always have to know the address of a page to view it. The wonderful thing about the Web is that you can access pages through the use of *hyperlinks*. You will notice that hyperlinks are often colored words (typically blue) on a Web page. Images may also be hyperlinks. Your mouse is used to select or click on the desired hyperlink. Some Web authors write their pages so that their hyperlinks are hidden from you. If you aren't sure where the hyperlinks are, just click on everything. You can't break anything. Clicking on a hyperlink will take you to a new Web page just as typing in an address does.

Here are a few more places you might find both fun and interesting.

The Map Machine from National Geographic
http://www.nationalgeographic.com/resources/ngo/maps

CIA Publications and Handbooks
http://www.odci.gov/cia/publications/pubs.html

The Coin-Operated Congress
http://bsd.mojones.com/coinop_congress/

MTV Online
http://www.mtv.com/

A Guide to Health Care Reform for Young Americans
http://www.iuma.com/RTV//

Macarena Lessons
http://www.nsmi.com/macarena

Experiment with each of the toolbar buttons on your browser. Remember that you can always use your *Back*, *Forward*, or *Home* buttons to retrace your steps.

The author of a Web page can connect *one* image to *many* different places. This type of hyperlink is sometimes called a *clickable map*. For example, think of a Web page with a map of the United States. The creator of this map could place a hyperlink within the boundary of each state on the map so that your selection would take you to information about that state. For a little experience in using this type of navigation, visit the sites in the following box.

> Here are five addresses that use clickable maps. They are also good places to find helpful information on political science topics.
>
> **Environmental Protection Agency**
> http://www.epa.gov
>
> **Map Stats**
> http://www.census.gov/datamap/www/index.html
>
> **Social Science Data Archives—Europe**
> http://www.nsd.uib.no/cessda/europe.html
>
> **Socioeconomic Data and Application Center**
> http://sedac.ciesin.org/
>
> **Earth Resources Observation Systems**
> http://edcwww.cr.usgs.gov/eros-home.html
>
> Not all browsers support clickable maps. Most experienced Web authors, however, provide conventional hyperlinks to related sites in addition to the clickable map.

Some Web pages contain *forms*. A form is generally a request for information, which you may respond to by clicking with your mouse or typing an answer. Forms can be used to survey users, answer questions, or make requests. As the box below shows, you can obtain valuable information from companies, government agencies, or educational institutions.

> Experiment with the following links that involve forms. Not all browsers support forms, so you will need to determine if yours does.
>
> **On the Job**
> http://voter.cq.com/cq_job.htm
>
> **Federal Information Exchange, Inc.**
> http://www.fie.com/
>
> **The Great American Website**
> http://www.uncle-sam.com/
>
> **FindLaw**
> http://www.findlaw.com/

Section 2.2
Landmarks—Navigating

The Internet addresses that you've been using are also called *Uniform Resource Locators*, or *URLs*. Each URL (pronounced "earl") has a couple of basic parts just like a residential address. Look at some of the URLs that you've used already. Do you notice any similarities among them?

> Here is another typical URL (this will take you to a pretty cool site). The three basic components of an URL are listed below the address. Compare this one to the others you've seen so far.
>
> http://lcweb.loc.gov/homepage/lchp.html
>
> **protocol** http://
> **server**   lcweb.loc.gov
> **path**   /homepage/lchp.html
>
> You may notice that some addresses don't have a path element—this information is not always necessary. Be careful when you type an URL. Even one incorrect letter will prevent the browser from finding the desired site. Here is an additional resource if you'd like to learn more about Internet addresses:
>
> http://www.ncsa.uiuc.edu/demoweb/url-primer.html

Now pick up any recent magazine and leaf through the articles and advertisements. With little effort you should be able to recognize a few more URLs. Just as you might recognize a string of numbers to be a phone number (e.g., 555-1212), you should be able to spot URLs by their characteristic form and order. An URL may seem confusing at first glance, but think of it as a postal address strung together without any spaces.

The *protocol* of the URL indicates how the information is stored. In the last box, http refers to the protocol, or language, that is used by all Web servers. The colon and slashes are used to separate it from the name of the server. They are not necessarily present in every type of URL. The *path* describes the location of the Web page on the server.

> Up to this point, we have only been discussing browsers as way of navigating through information using hyperlinks. However, browsers also have

the power to link to other, much older, formats of information. Try the following URLs to notice how the information differs.

>   ftp://sri.com/netinfo/interest-groups.txt
>   gopher://gopher.marvel.loc.gov/

HTTP, FTP, and Gopher are not the only protocols, but they are the three you're most likely to encounter. Have you ever encountered the following Internet protocols?

telnet://

wais://

news:

A domain is just a fancy name for a functional network group. The last part of the server name defines the domain to which the server belongs. The most common domain is indicated by the letters edu; all educational institutions are members of this domain group. Another important domain is com, which stands for commercial and includes Internet servers that belong to **commercial** companies. You are also likely to encounter domains that serve other groups; abbreviations for a few of these are shown below.

> Here are some URLs that may help expand your understanding of domains. Can you determine what each domain group represents?
>
>   http://www.apsanet.org/
>   http://www.aarp.org/
>   http://www.nasa.gov
>   http://www.nra.org/
>   http://www.envirolink.org

In your travels, you will eventually jump to a server that is outside your country. Much, but not all, of the information on these servers is in English. URLs of servers outside the United States have an additional section at the end of the server name. It is a two letter code that indicates the country. Here are just a few examples of the many you might find. (All the country codes are listed in **http://www.ics.uci.edu/pub/websoft/wwwstat/country-codes.txt**

- .au   Australia
- .ca   Canada
- .ch   Switzerland
- .nl   Netherlands
- .lt   Lithuania
- .pe   Peru
- .uk   United Kingdom

> Here is yet another opportunity to encounter new places on the Web. It is a directory that allows you to search for specific things. This group of tools is discussed later in the chapter, but you might want to play with it first.
>
> **Yahoo!**
> http://www.yahoo.com

Return Visit

Now that you've found a number of interesting pages, how do you find them again a day or a week later? Your browser provides a way to mark an intriguing site and quickly return to it. Netscape calls this feature *Bookmarks* (see Figure 2.2). By using such a feature, you can compile a list of pages you frequently visit. When you wish to return to one of these pages, you simply select it from the list by clicking on it with your mouse. You will jump directly to the site.

Here is an URL to get your collection started. Try this address: **http://www.hotwired.com**. It's a pretty interesting place: the online version of Wired Magazine. If you have Netscape, select *Add Bookmark* from the *Bookmarks* menu (see Figure 2.2). Later on, if you use your mouse to select the *Bookmarks* menu, you'll see that *Hotwired* is just a jump away. Thus, you don't have to memorize the URL or haphazardly jump around until you find it again.

Figure 2.2. As pages are added to this list they will appear at the bottom of this same pull-down menu.

Now that you've got the hang of it, give the following URLs a try.

Political Science Virtual Library
http://spirit.lib.uconn.edu/PoliSci/polisci.htm

Webliography
http://www.lib.lsu.edu/weblio.html

Surf the Best Websites
http://www.pointcom.com/

Political Science Resources on the Web
http://www.lib.umich.edu/libhome/Documents.center/polisci.html

World Lecture Hall
http://www.utexas.edu/world/lecture/index.html

TicketMaster Online
http://www.ticketmaster.com

The Federal Web Locator
http://www.law.vill.edu/Fed-Agency/fedwebloc.html

The United Nations
http://www.un.org/

Project Vote Smart
http://www.vote-smart.org/

Bartlett's Familiar Quotations
http://www.columbia.edu/acis/bartleby/bartlett/

American Voter
http://voter96.cqalert.com/

Weird Sites
http://www.euronet.nl/users/deiman/index.html

Political Chat
http://www.4-lane.com/politicalchat/

Alphabetical List of Political Links
http://www1.mhv.net/~btuchman/links.html

LSU Political Science Resources
http://www.lsu.edu/guests/poli/public_html/polires2.html

The Skeptic's Dictionary
http://wheel.ucdavis.edu/~btcarrol/skeptic/dictcont.html

When you find something that you think is fun and interesting, save it or give the address to a friend.

As you begin to accumulate more sites on your list, you'll notice how cluttered and disorganized they can become. In addition to the ability to collect Web addresses, most browsers also allow you to organize them as you desire. Refer to Figure 2.2 and notice the menu option immediately below the *Add . . .* feature. This option, called *Go to Bookmarks*, allows you to organize your Web address list. When you select this option, a small window will open; in it you can move and manipulate your list of Web addresses.

Travel History

If you've been working along with your manual and browser at the same time, you've probably been to many places on the Web. If you want to move back and forth between your selections, you're probably using the *Forward* and *Back* buttons on the browser toolbar. But what do you do if you want to go back to some place you've visited fifteen jumps ago? Do you press the *Back* button fifteen times? Well, it works, but it's a little slow. You might want to try a new feature: It allows you to jump rapidly to any of the places you've visited along your path of travel. In *Navigator*, select the *Go* menu. You'll see a list of all of the places you've visited on your journey. To jump to a site on the list, simply click/select the site with your mouse. With *Navigator*, you'll also find a similar feature called *History* under the *Windows* menu. By selecting *History*, you'll open a new window listing the names *and* the URLs for all of the places you've visited recently. Other browsers have similar features.

Because the list compiled under *Go* or *History* begin anew each time you start your browser, you should use *Bookmarks* when you find something interesting.

Section 2.3
Asking for directions—Searching

The Internet is full of valuable information, but it's not always easy to find what you need. A number of easy-to-use tools are available for free. With practice, these tools will help you develop your information-finding skills.

There are two types of tools that you'll use most often to search for information. These are *Directories* and *Search Engines*.

Directories

Yahoo! (**http://www.yahoo.com**) is only one of many directories that are available on the Internet, but it is the best one available for general topics. (The name Yahoo is taken from Jonathan Swift's *Gulliver's Travels*, which describes a Yahoo as a crude, uncivilized, and according to one of *Yahoo's* founders, an interesting person.)

Yahoo! began as a simple listing of information by category, kind of like a card catalog. In the last few years, it has added the ability to search for specific information. At the top level of the directory, there are several very general categories, but as you move deeper into the directory you'll notice that the categories become more specific. To find information, you simply choose the most appropriate category at the top level and continue through each successive level until you find what you're looking for (or until you realize you're in the wrong place). It's not unusual to get lost. In such cases, just begin again and try different categories.

Suppose that you are interested in obtaining information about the amount of military or welfare spending in this year's fiscal budget of the United States. What does *Yahoo!* Have to say about this topic? We find that one of the top-level categories in *Yahoo!* is Governmnent. Within the Government category a number of general political areas are listed, including U.S. Government. For the moment we choose the U.S. Government subcategory. Eureka! In the U.S. Government subcategory we find a cross-reference to Budget. If we had chosen Politics at the Government juncture and then selected Political Issues, U.S. Budget would be cross-referenced. Because *Yahoo!* Cross-references among the categories, you will find that several related categories will lead to the information you desire.

Much of your success in finding information when using a directory like *Yahoo!* depends upon your preparation for the search. Often, it is possible to find information on a topic in a category that may at first seem unrelated to your topic of interest. Let's take the example of tax reform. Are you especially interested in reforming the Internal Revenue Service? If so, you might search under the *Yahoo!* subcategory of Economy. (In *Yahoo!*, Tax Law is a subcategory of Taxes, which in turn is a subcategory of the top-level Economy category.) In the sub-category Federal try the links provided to find information about The Taxpayer Relief Act.

Prepare yourself for a search *before* you jump into one. In the long run, it will save you both time and frustration. Don't be afraid to try some unusual approaches in your search strategy. A good technique is to pull out your thesaurus and look up other names for the topic you're searching. Think of everything associated with your question and give each of these possibilities a try. You never know what might turn up a gold mine.

Search Engines

A more direct approach to finding information on the Web is to use a *search engine*, which is a program that runs a search while you wait for the results. Many search engines can be found on the Web. Some of Web search engines are commercial and may charge you a fee to run a search. Search engines are also available for other parts of the Internet: *Archie*, *Veronica*, and *Jughead* are examples of such search engines.

Alta Vista (**http://www.altavista.digital.com**) offers general and detailed searches through what Digital Equipment Corporation claims is the largest Web index. According to Alta Vista, the user can search billions of words found in millions of Web pages. In addition, you can access a full-text index of more than 13,000 newsgroups.

Excite! (**http://www.excite.com**) is very versatile because it tracks down information by searching for concepts, not just keywords. Suppose, for example, that you're interested in human radiation experiments conducted by the U.S. Government immediately after World War II. *Excite!* can find such information even though the source presents information on the medical uses of radiation, for example. *Excite!* provides you with a percentage of how close it "thinks" it came to providing pertinent information on your concept(s). In addition, *Excite!* has such capabilities as finding a specific news article from newsgroups by a text search.

InfoSeek Guide (**http://guide.infoseek.com**) is a search/browse service that returns both search hits and a list of topics related to your search. With each search, you get the most relevant matches, related topics to explore, and current news and views from popular magazines, TV networks, and online experts. *InfoSeek Guide* also helps you find email addresses, stock quotes, company profiles, and other materials.

A frequently used search engine is *Lycos* (**http://www.lycos.com**). It's simple to operate but, as with any search tool, it takes practice and patience to master. Take the time now to connect to *Lycos*, and we'll take it for a test run. The instructions on the opening page will tell you almost everything you need to know. To search, enter a word into the white text entry box and press the submit button. *Lycos* will refer back to its database of information and return a page of hyperlinked resources containing the word you entered. When the query results come back to you, notice that they are hyperlinks to various sites on the Internet.

To see how a search engine works, use "tax reform" for search. Observe that you can set the number of responses that the engine will return to you. Did you also notice that some of your results did not seem to apply to your topic? Regardless of which search engine you use, remember that they are all fast but dumb. A search using the "tax reform" will also turn up a link to A Theory of Tax Reform in Developing Countries. To perform an effective search, you will need to spend time before the search preparing a search strategy. When you do research using an automated tool like a search engine, you can expect many links to be unrelated to your topic. Continuous research in advanced computing will undoubtedly result in smarter search engines. Until then, the most intelligent re-searcher is at the keyboard. Despite some misses, you'll find that search engines are very powerful tools and will save you time in the long run.

One last comment on search engines: these tools don't directly search the Internet. They actually search a database that is derived from the Internet. Here is how it works. Initially, information robots (automated programming tools) sift and categorize information on the Internet and place it into a database. It is this database that is inspected when you use a search engine. Therefore, each search engine is only as effective as its cadre of robots that generate the database. Thus it is wise not to rely on just one search engine. Use several, because what one does not find, another might.

Here's a way to test the skills you've developed from your accumulated Internet experience. Using *Yahoo!* and *Lycos* (or any of the other search tools described in this chapter) find information on the Web related to the words given below. Compare the results with searches using the additional resources provided at the bottom of this box. The last three resources (MetaCrawler, Findspot, and Search.com) allow you to choose from a collection of search tools.

Affirmative Action   Apportionment
Campaign Finance Reform   Executive Privilege
Judicial Activism   Line-Item Veto

WebCrawler
  http://www.webcrawler.com

BigFoot
  http://www.bigfoot.com

HotBot
  http://www.hotbot.com

MetaCrawler
  http://www.metacrawler.com

Finspot
  http://www.findspot.com

Search.com
  http://www.search.com

Activity:
The Great Cybertrip

Obtaining information on the Web is easy. It may be somewhat harder to find the *right* information, however. Discovering the correct information is still exciting and interesting, not unlike getting lost and finding your way again in an unfamiliar city. The first list is a set of some commonly-heard terms in Political Science. See what you can find on these topics. How have each of these terms enhanced our understanding of our political life?

- Popular Sovereignty
- Flat Tax
- Sexual Harassment
- Executive Order
- Health Care Reform
- Social Security Reform
- Unfunded Mandate
- Budget Deficit
- Separation of Powers
- Realignment

Understanding Political Science often means learning about the women and men who have made significant contributions in both theory and methodology. Below is a short list of some pioneering thinkers in Political Science. Some of them will be very easy to track down while other will not. We hope you'll find both their perspectives and their lives interesting.

Your assignment, should you accept it, is to put together a brief history of the Political Philosophers/Scientists listed below and their important contributions. If you want more of a challenge, suggest four substitutions and explain the reasons for your choices.

- Plato
- Thomas Hobbes
- Machiavelli
- John Locke
- Alexis de Tocqueville
- James Madison
- Adam Smith
- Karl Marx
- Walter Lippman
- John Maynard Keynes
- V.O. Key
- Harold Laswell
- Walter Dean Burnham
- C. Wright Mills
- Max Weber
- John Dewey
- Martin Luther King
- Theodore Lowi

Remember to use all of the resources at your disposal. Begin with *Yahoo!* and then move to the other search engines. Check the obscure as well as the popular resources. You are also welcome to read ahead to Chapter 3, which explains how to use e-mail and newsgroups. These resources may be helpful, too.

Chapter 3
Traveling in Style
As You Like It

We shape our tools and afterwards our tools shape us.

By now you have probably wandered through some of the many resources offered on the Web. In this chapter we will cover additional techniques to make your Web experience more enjoyable and beneficial.

Section 3.1
Coffee, tea, or milk? Customizing

On the Internet, saving time is critical if you have to use a modem and an Internet Service Provider (ISP) to cruise the Net. If you know what your browser can and cannot do, and if you configure the options for your browser so that it is most efficient for you, you will save both time and money. Try the modifications described below as you read; also, feel free to jump to the information that is most important to you.

With *Navigator*, you have several ways to customize the appearance and behavior of your browser. These customizing features are known as *Options*. Descriptions for some of the *Options* follow, as well as the reasons you might want to change them. After you investigate *Options*, you'll be able to explore the other custom features on your own.

> Some of you may want a more detailed description of your Netscape browser. Netscape has included access to a detailed set of descriptions and instructions on its homepage. To access the Netscape *Navigator Handbook*, select *Help* from the menu bar and choose *Handbook* from the menu list.

> This will connect you to Netscape's online handbook. Because this information is online and not held within your browser, you need an active Internet connection to use it. You can access this same information from the following URL:
>
> http://home.netscape.com/eng/mozilla/3.0/handbook/

Setting Options

Navigator lists common functions under the *Options* menu on the menu bar at the top of the window. Select *Options* and a pull-down window will appear (Figure 3.1). Notice that there are check marks by some of the options. Look at *Auto Load Images*, for example. When there is a check mark (✓), images will be loaded automatically. If you select this option again, the check mark disappears and subsequently pages will load the text without the time-consuming images. Give it a try. *Navigator* lists only the basic options here. Experiment with the other basic options (each of these begin with *Show*) to see what they do.

Additional options can be accessed from one of the *Preference. . .* submenus. (You can see these at the top of the *Options* pull-down menu.) Once you've selected one of *Navigator's Preferences. . .* windows, you'll notice that the preferences are broken down into categories according to function (Figure 3.2). The different categories are listed at the top of the window; they look like tabs in a file folder. As we describe different customizing options, we will refer to *both* the specific preference window and the specific tab within that window (i.e., *General Preferences. . .* window and *Appearance* tab).

Now that you know where to go to modify the setup for your browser,

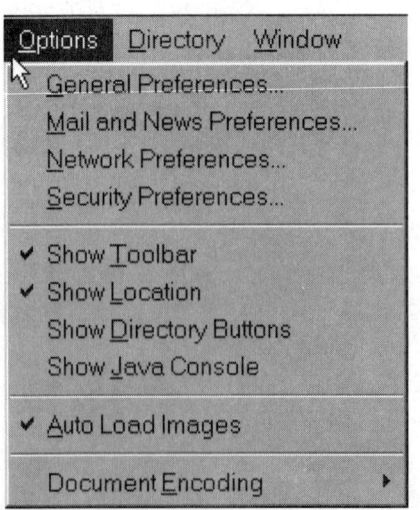

Figure 3.1. For Netscape *Navigator*, many of the general options are listed near the bottom of the *Options* menu. If you want to set specific options, you can select the different *Preferences. . .* available at the top of the box.

Figure 3.2. These are the *General Preferences* categories in *Navigator*. This illustration includes only the categories and not the contents of the window. The contents will vary depending on the tab selection. A different set of tabs and categories exist for each of the different *Preferences* windows.

we'll describe some of the features you may want to modify. You will probably want to look at each preference even if you choose not to modify it. Also, keep in mind that some of these changes are not relevant to your setup; others require specific information in order for your browser to work with your ISP. You can always check the online *Navigator Handbook* for help.

Homepage

You might want to modify the location of your homepage. A homepage is like "home" in a game of hopscotch. It is the place you begin hopping from square to square. If you're working with a browser that hasn't been customized before, the company that made the browser probably chose the homepage. If you're working on one of your school's computers, then the homepage may already be set to the school's page. If you're permitted to change the homepage, then decide what you want to designate as your homepage. By now you've probably found something on the Web that you are willing to call home. When *your* homepage is properly set, every time you start your browser or select *Home* from the toolbar, you'll end up at this place. Later in this chapter, we'll discuss how you can make and display your own homepage.

In *Navigator*, open the *Options* menu, choose the *General Preferences* window and then select the *Appearance* tab. At the center of the window you will see a dialog box within the *Startup* control panel (Figure 3.3) that allows you to set your homepage. Type in the URL of your new homepage.

Figure 3.3. On *Navigator*, the *Startup* control panel within the *Appearance* tab of the *General Preferences* includes a dialog box that will allow you to enter the URL for your desired homepage.

Linkage

You have probably noticed that hyperlinks are normally blue (unless someone has changed the default color). Once you've accessed the page that the hyperlink represents, it changes to purple. Think of this as the bread crumb principle. The purple links remind you that you've already been down a particular path (link) and that you might want to select a different path. Eventually, however, the hyperlink will change back to its default color. But you can designate the elapsed time before a hyperlink changes back to the default color. You can also choose the default color. Generally, the more time you spend on the Internet, the more quickly (within 24 hours, for example) your links should revert to default. If you travel frequently and find that your hyperlinks are always purple, then your expiration limit may be set too long.

From the *Options* menu, open the *General Preferences* window and select the *Appearance* tab. At the bottom of the window, you will see a dialog box that allows you to set the length of time in days for hyperlinks to expire (Figure 3.4).

Font Style, Size, and Color

If you spend a great deal of time on the computer, then you realize the importance of adjusting your monitor, desk, and keyboard to minimize potential eye strain and muscle fatigue. Selecting a font of appropriate color, style, and size should help alleviate the hazard.

To change the default style and size of the font, select the *Options* menu and open the *General Preferences* window. Select the *Font* tab from this window (Figure 3.5). You may modify the default settings for both the font size and style used by your browser.

To view other possible font settings, select the appropriate *Choose Font...* button. You should work primarily with the proportional font setting because it is used for the normal text on your browser. (Fixed fonts are generally used when a page designer is illustrating computer code or text requiring uniform spacing.) A small window will appear; in it you can select from numerous font styles and sizes. When you click the OK button, those font settings will be selected as the default for your browser. If you like your selection, click the OK button at the bottom of the *Fonts* tab window.

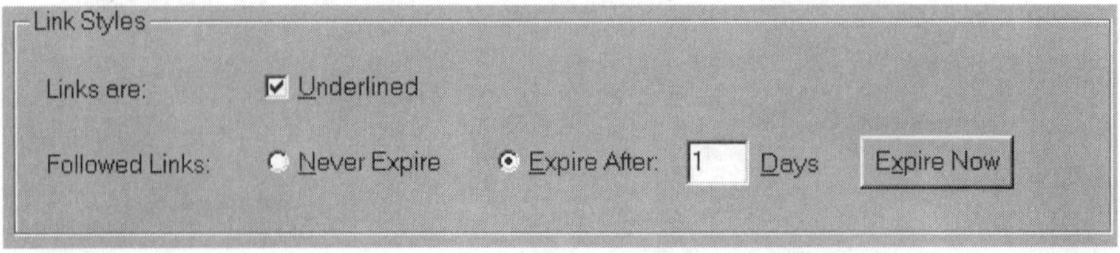

Figure 3.4. On *Navigator*, the *Link Styles* control panel within the *General Preferences* tab group allows you to control the appearance and behavior of hyperlinks.

Figure 3.5. On *Navigator*, the *Fonts* tab group within the *General Preferences* option window allows you to choose the default font size and style of text elements.

To change the default colors, select the *Options* menu and open the *General Preferences* window. Select the *Colors* tab from this window (Figure 3.6). You may modify the default color settings used by your browser for the hyperlinks (*Links* and *Followed Links*) and regular text containing no hyperlinks (*Text*). (*Links* refer to unvisited links, whereas *Followed Links* refer to links already selected.)

To change the color setting, select the appropriate *Choose Color...* button. A small window will appear displaying numerous color choices. When you select the *OK* button, that color will be selected as your custom color. If you like your choice, click the OK button in the *Colors* tab window.

Experiment with the *Colors* tab window. Try to modify both the text and background colors. Also, try to discover how you might use an image in the background instead of a solid color. Remember not to go overboard with your

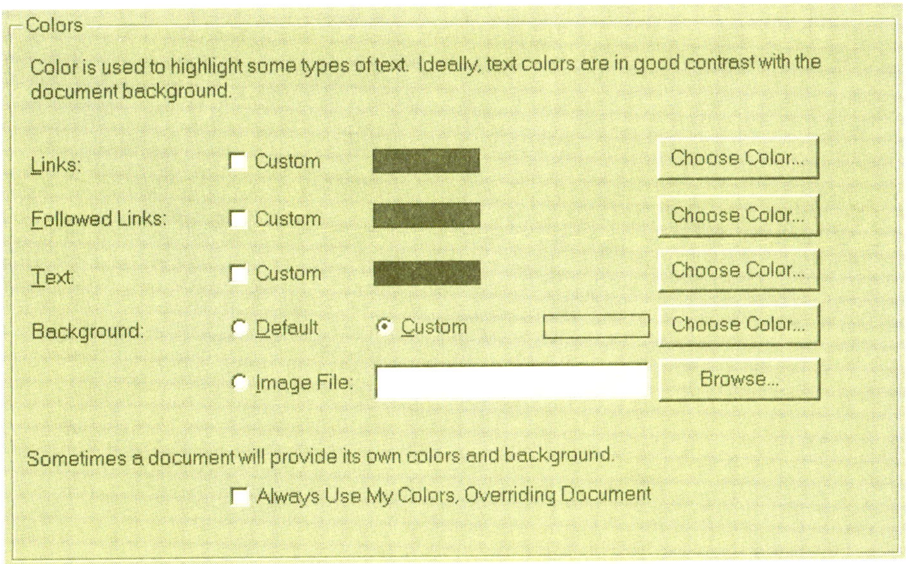

Figure 3.6. On *Navigator*, the *Colors* control panel within the *General Preferences* option group allows you to choose the default colors of hypertext and text elements.

power; you still need to be able to read the words on the page. Some font colors or sizes may be difficult to read and may cause more eye strain.

Although we have not discussed all of the options, you probably have enough information to understand how to use them. Experiment with the settings on your own. You can always check the online *Navigator Handbook* for help. If you are using Microsoft *Internet Explorer* or another browser, you will find that they have very similar features.

Section 3.2
Wish you were here—Communicating

Navigator and most other browsers allow you to communicate through e-mail, newsgroups, and online interest groups. E-mail links are built into many Web pages and enable you to send correspondence directly to other people through the Internet.

E-mail

E-mail is the electronic exchange of mail among people. This exchange is from one person to one (or more) specified people. Like web browsers and web servers, e-mail operates according to a Client-Server model. Your client software asks a server computer for mail addressed to you. Your mail server is operated and maintained by the administrator of your campus or ISP. Although your Web server speaks a computer protocol called HyperText Transport Protocol (HTTP), your mail server speaks a computer protocol called Simple Mail Transport Protocol (SMTP).

Think of the server as your mailbox. The mailbox is where mail addressed to you is stored until you pick it up. You use your mail client to retrieve your mail from your mailbox.

Gaining access to an e-mail server is easy. If you are at a campus that has provided you with Internet access, you should be able to apply for an e-mail account through your campus computer administrator. Otherwise, you can apply for an e-mail account through an ISP. If you use an ISP to access the Internet, you probably have e-mail capabilities. In order to properly configure your browser for sending e-mail, you need to know (1) your e-mail address and (2) the name of your mail server.

Before configuring the browser for e-mail, let's look at the form of an e-mail address: NAME@HOST.DOMAIN. It is not necessary to have a full name for the NAME part of the address; in fact, some addresses use only numbers.

The @ symbol in e-mail addresses is known simply as the "at" symbol. Around the world, it is known by more colorful names. For example, in Italy and in France it is known as "chiocciolina" and "petit escargot" (little snail); in the Netherlands it's "api" (short for apestaart, monkey's tail); in Norway it's "kariel-bolle" (a twisted cinnamon bun); in Denmark it's "snabel A" (an A with a trunk); in Germany it's "Klammeraffe" (spider monkey); and in Finland it's called "miau" (for another animal with a tail).

Here are two typical e-mail addresses.

puetzj@nhmccd.edu

vjbenok@sheperd.wvnet.edu

The three basic components of an e-mail address include

user name	puetzj	vjbenok
host server	nhmccd	shepherd.wvnet
domain	edu	edu

Drop us a note if you have any comments about this manual.

Your *User Name* is also the NAME associated with your e-mail address. The @ symbol always follows the NAME and then the name of the server computer (HOST). The domain in the e-mail format, just like the domain of the URL format, is used to indicate the affiliation of the user. Notice that there are no spaces anywhere in an e-mail address. Sometimes dashes, periods, or underscores are used as separators in e-mail addresses. Also, e-mail addresses are not case sensitive, so you can capitalize letters or not at your discretion.

Your campus computer administrator or your ISP will provide you with an e-mail address. This is the address you'll give to your friends. It will also be posted with any correspondence you send on the Internet.

Configuring your browser to send and receive e-mail only takes two steps.

First: To set your personal information, select the *Options* menu and open the *Mail and News Preferences* window. Select the *Identity* tab and you will see the text entry boxes where you can enter your information (Figure 3.7).

Second: To set your e-mail information, select the *Options* menu and open the *Mail and News Preferences* window. Select the *Servers* tab and you will see the text entry boxes (Figure 3.8). After you've entered the correct information, restart the browser program. Now you should have the ability to send and receive e-mail. Think about it! You'll save on postage and long-distance phone bills.

Most e-mail systems use a single machine to handle both incoming and outgoing mail. However, some systems use a different machine for incoming and outgoing mail. In Figure 3.8, note that two different text entry boxes are

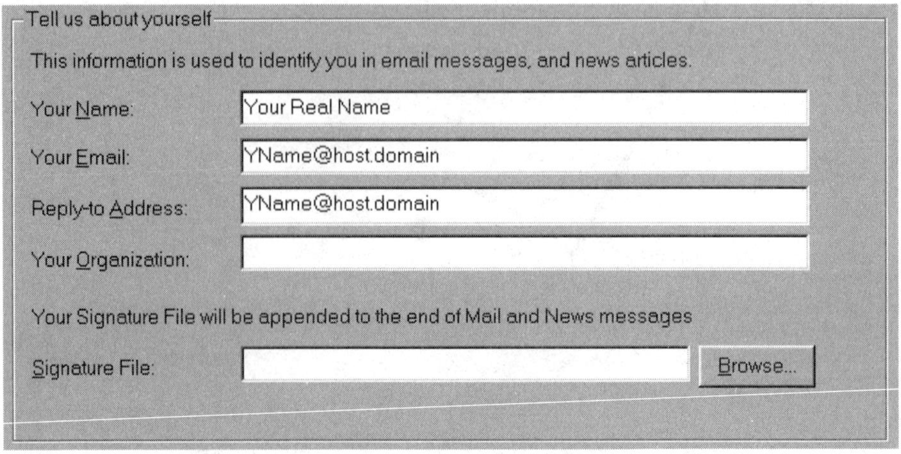

[Tell us about yourself]

This information is used to identify you in email messages, and news articles.

Your Name: `Your Real Name`
Your Email: `YName@host.domain`
Reply-to Address: `YName@host.domain`
Your Organization:

Your Signature File will be appended to the end of Mail and News messages

Signature File: [   ] [Browse...]

Figure 3.7. This information helps to identify you when you send e-mail. Use the *Signature* feature to place standard information (such as your address and phone number) at the bottom of your messages.

provided for the mail server. If your system uses just one machine, enter the mail server twice. The person who sets up your account should be able to give you all the information you need. If they are less than helpful, then it is generally safe to assume that the address for both your incoming and outgoing mail server is MAIL.HOST.DOMAIN.

Now let's send some e-mail. Select the *Windows* option from the menu bar and choose *Netscape Mail*. A new window will open (Figure 3.9).

Notice that this window is similar to a Web browser. (It is also similar to the news reader that we will discuss later.) To view your mail, select the *Get Mail* button. If you have mail, then it will appear on the left side of the

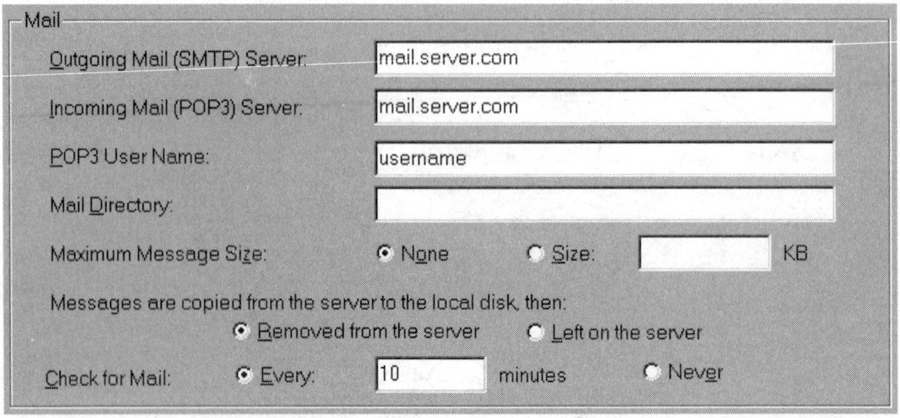

[Mail]

Outgoing Mail (SMTP) Server: `mail.server.com`
Incoming Mail (POP3) Server: `mail.server.com`
POP3 User Name: `username`
Mail Directory:
Maximum Message Size: ⦿ None   ○ Size: [   ] KB
Messages are copied from the server to the local disk, then:
    ⦿ Removed from the server   ○ Left on the server
Check for Mail: ⦿ Every: [10] minutes   ○ Never

Figure 3.8. The information about your particular mail server and e-mail address must be entered before you can receive e-mail from others through *Navigator*.

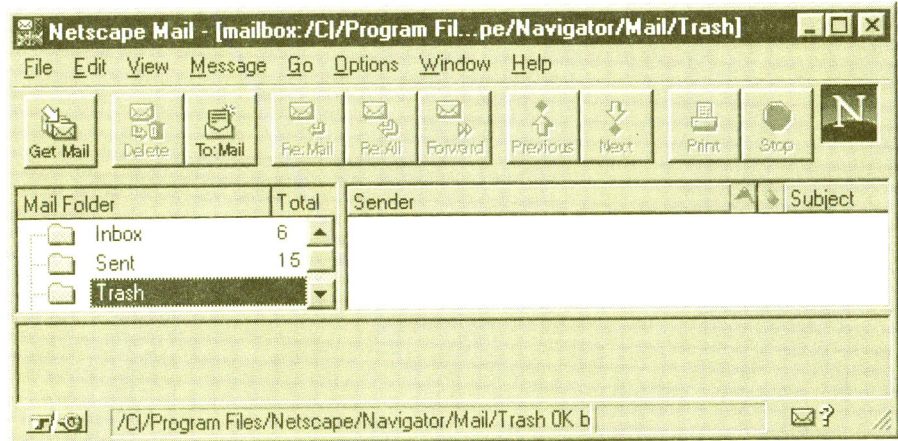

Figure 3.9. *Navigator* includes a built-in mail client. Its features are similar to those of a Web browser.

window. All incoming mail arrives in the *Inbox*. When you select the *Inbox*, its contents will appear on the right side of the window. When you select a specific mail item you will see the contents displayed at the bottom of the window. To test the setup, send yourself an e-mail message. Next, write your congressperson. You can find his/her address in the box below.

Now that you've got the basics down, here are three sites you'll find useful.

A Beginner's Guide to Effective Email
http://www.webfoot.com/advice/email.top.html

The Electronic Activist
http://www.ifas.org/activist/index.html

Congressional E-mail Directory
http://www.webslingerz.com/jhoffman/congress-email.html

Newsgroups

Many browsers enable users to exchange ideas by using newsgroups. A newsgroup is a group of people who participate in a specialized discussion on the Internet. These groups are open forums in which all are welcomed to contribute. Newsgroup postings are sent to a common place for all to read and reply. Some are moderated by one or more people who post items for discussion and referee any electronic brawls that may ensue. However, not all newsgroups are rife with disagreement. Many offer excellent opportunities for polite conversation with courteous people. All newsgroups provide a place where people can bring new ideas and perspectives to the screen. If e-mail is like the postal service, though, newsgroups are like coffee houses on open microphone night.

What is the purpose of the newsgroups if people just contribute ideas and comments on a particular subject? Newsgroups are places where you can ask questions, get ideas, and learn about specific topics. Select a group that has an interest common to yours or a topic that you are trying to learn about. You'll find that there are many newsgroups that focus on Political Science and government-related areas.

The names of newsgroups usually describe their discussion topic. There are several major newsgroup categories. The ones you'll probably use most are the ALT, GOV, SCI, SOC, REC, and TALK groups. Political topics may be found in nearly all of these newsgroup categories. Other newsgroups include COMP.SOCIETY for topics specific to computers and social responsibility, SOC.SUPPORT for people coping with depression or family crises. The ALT group is generally used for alternative topics that typically encompass controversial social, economic, political, or religious ideas. We've included a list of relevant newsgroups in Appendix II. You'll find some of them interesting and helpful as a supplement to your studies in the Humanities and Social Sciences.

Here is a typical newsgroup URL. Newsgroup names are divided into several descriptive words separated by a period and organized according to a hierarchy. Note that newsgroup URLs don't use the double slash (//).

alt.politics.media

Here are the main components:

protocol   news:
    top category   alt
        sub category   politics
            sub category   media

To configure your browser to connect to a newsgroup, you will need the name of the server computer that handles newsgroups. (Get this from the same people who gave you your mail server address.) You'll perform almost the same procedure you used to set up your e-mail service. To set your newsgroup information, select the *Options* menu and open the *Mail and News Preferences* window. Select the *Servers* tab and you will see the text entry boxes (Figure 3.10). Once you enter the correct information and restart the browser program, you should be able to view newsgroups. You may find that you can't access some newsgroups. Check to make sure your ISP subscribes to these groups. If not, your ISP will usually do so if you make a request.

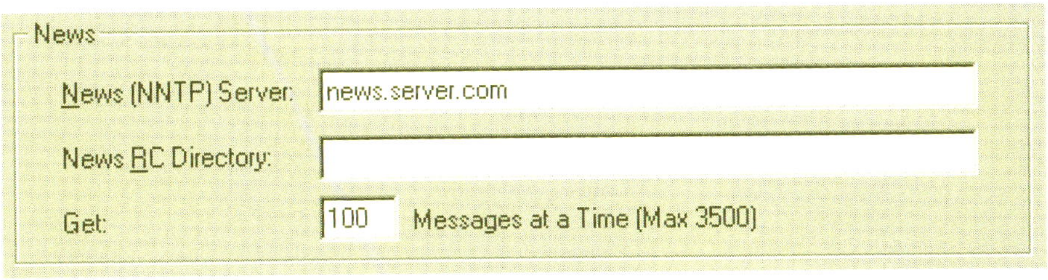

Figure 3.10. With *Navigator*, the dialog window where you will enter the name of your news server can be found in *Mail and News Preferences...* option under the *Options* menu.

News servers use a protocol called *NetNews Transfer Protocol*, or NNTP. You might need to ask around to find out the address for your news server. If you can't find someone to help, you can probably assume that the address for your news server is NEWS.HOST.DOMAIN.

You should now be ready for an adventure. When you use *Navigator* to read or post articles to newsgroups, you won't be using the same window that you used for browsing the Web. For newsgroups, you'll use what is typically called a *news reader*. To start your news reader, select the *Windows* option from the menu bar and choose *Netscape News*. A new window will open (Figure 3.11).

Note how this window resembles the Web browser, as well as how it differs. To view a larger list of newsgroups you can select *Options* from the menu bar and choose *Show All Newsgroups*. A larger list of newsgroups will appear on the left. You can subscribe to a specific one by placing a check mark by the desired newsgroup. When you select a newsgroup, the individual articles will appear on the right side of the window. Finally, when you select a specific article, you will see the contents displayed at the bottom of the news reader window. Now, take some time and explore.

Figure 3.11. *Navigator* includes a built-in news reader. Its features are similar to both the mail client and the Web browser.

> The only way to really understand what newsgroups are like is to try them. Here are a several newsgroups that will get you started. Connect to one of interest and read some of the postings. For your first time, you should just read the postings and follow some of the conversations. (This is called lurking.) Connections or threads develop between postings as people add comments to earlier postings. As you become familiar with the topic of discussion, you might post a comment yourself. Before you jump in, you may want to read the section titled "Language for the Road" in this chapter.
>
>
>
> **alt.politics.clinton**
> **alt.politics.democrats**
> **alt.politics.republicans**
> **gov.us.fed.congress.bills.house**
> **alt.conspiracy.right-wing**
>
>
>
> Two useful tools for newsgroups are *DejaNews* and *Reference.com*. *DejaNews* (**http://www/dejanews.com/**) allows you to search for topics in newsgroups. *Reference.com* (**http://www.reference.com/**) notifies you by e-mail if topics specified by you are discussed. Take a look at both of these!

Chat

This is yet another avenue for communication. It is probably the one you'll choose if you like to talk. Unlike e-mail and newsgroups, which require you to wait for a response, chat rooms are real-time. This means that you are conversing and observing conversations as they happen. As with newsgroups, it is best to observe the interactions of several chat rooms and read the new user information before you jump in. Some rooms can be excessive and vulgar, but many are frequented by polite people with a genuine desire for conversation. Just like newsgroups, chat rooms are organized by topic and you can usually anticipate the discussion by the name of the group. Unlike newsgroups, there are few academic-specific chat rooms; therefore, you'll probably find that they are a great place for general conversation.

> Just to get you started, here are a few Web-based chat groups. Read the instructions and ask for help if you need it.
>
> **Chat Politics**
>   http://www.chatpolitics.com/

Conservatism, Libertarianism, and Liberalism Live Chat
http://mobydicks.com/commons/Conservatism,Libertarianism,andhall/live/chat.cgi

WBS Chat-Politics
http://webchat9.wbs.net/webchat3.so?cmd=cmd_doorway:talk.politics.misc

Unlike e-mail and newsgroups, you will be frequently asked to login or register before beginning to chat. Often you'll even be given a password. Always, read the rules for participating and ask for help if you don't understand something. The participants are generally very helpful. The other characteristic of chat rooms is that typically you will use a "handle" or pseudonym when you post a message.

Language for the Road

A few words of caution. Unlike normal conversations between people, electronic exchanges don't convey vocal inflections, facial expression, and body language. (These things aren't easily digitized and transmitted across a copper wire. To be sure, there are such things as Internet telephones and video conferencing, but for most of us they are not affordable and practical.) You will need to practice the way you communicate electronically and be patient when someone misinterprets something you've "said." For example, suppose you tell a joke. Because the reader only gets the text, she may think that you are serious and take offense. Computer people learned about this problem a long time ago and an innovative solution has been developed. The solution is a collection of "smileys."

Here are some smileys; tilt your head to the left to interpret them:

:-)	smile	:-x	my lips are sealed
:-)	wink	:-o	oh!
:-(	sad	:-l	indifferent
:-[	very sad	:-*	kiss

Because you will eventually get tired of typing all of the things you want to say, several acronyms are in common use. Here are a few:

BTW	By The Way
IMHO	In My Humble Opinion
FYI	For Your Information

FWIW   For What It's Worth
TIA   Thanks in Advance
ADN   Any Day Now
B4N   Bye For Now

Now for a couple of terms. Like any other culture, the Internet community has borrowed some common words to describe special situations. Here are two that you'll see:

Flame This refers to the act of yelling, insulting, or degrading a person or his or her character. You can expect to get flamed if you don't follow certain basic rules of netiquette (etiquette of the Net).
Spam This refers to the act of posting a comment, message, or advertisement to multiple newsgroups when the note doesn't really pertain to the newsgroup topic. It is the Internet equivalent of sending junk mail.

Here are a few Web resources that you will want to read when you begin communicating online. They are very helpful and entertaining. Enjoy!

E-Mail Etiquette
http://www.iwillfollow.com/email.htm

The Net: User Guidelines and Netiquette By Arlene H. Rinaldi
http://www.fav.edu/~rinaldi/net/index.htm

Electronic Frontier Foundation's Unofficial Smiley Dictionary
http://www.eff.org/papers/eegtti/eeg_286.html

Section 3.3
The fun is in the going—Extending

In early Web history, travel was pretty basic. The browser was a piece of software that acted as a totally self-contained vehicle. When you hooked it up, it contained everything you needed to cruise the Net. This has changed. As the Web grows larger, people develop new formats of information they wish to include on the Web. These new formats allow for a richer expression. Things like digital video, audio, animations, interactive games, and 3D worlds are currently very common on the Internet. As people demand more functionality from the Internet, new formats will become available. To cope with this continuing change, Netscape developed a way to add functionality without overloading the basic browser design.

Helpers and Plug-ins

Early Web pages included only text and images. They were much like brochures with the ability to hyperlink to other pages. The images that were included in Web pages were in a GIF format. However, to accommodate new image formats like JPEG, browsers turned to helper applications. If a page designer included a JPEG image, then an external helper application program displayed the image for viewing outside of the browser. Rather than having to rely on external programs, plug-in programs were developed to add the same features within the browser itself. For example, if you want to listen to music across the Internet from your browser, then you could install a plug-in that allows the browser to understand the audio format.

Netscape developed many plug-ins, and they are still the place to turn when you want one. An important thing, though: adding plug-ins to your browser will increase your memory (RAM) requirements. If you add too many plug-ins, your browser might stop working. Only install the plug-ins that you're going to use regularly.

These addresses will take you to the place where you can download the plug-ins to your computer. The developers also provide a very good description of how to install and use the plug-ins.

RealAudio by Progressive Networks
http://www.real.com/products/player/index.html

Shockwave by MacroMedia
http://www.macromedia.com/shockwave/download/

QuickTime by Apple
http://www.apple.com/quicktime

Once you've added a plug-in or two, you can get a list of the ones you've installed right from your browser. Select the *Help* menu and then choose *About Plug-ins*. The browser window will then present a list of all of your installed plug-ins. If you click on the link at the top of the page, you will also be able to connect directly to Netscape's master plug-in page.

Java and JavaScript

Grab a cup of coffee for this one. Helper application programs (helpers) and plug-ins weren't enough to satisfy Web developers. Web developers wanted even more—*more* flexibility, *more* interactivity, and *more* control. *Java* and *JavaScript* were developed to provide the more that developers wanted. But to understand what Java and JavaScript are, you need to understand what Web pages *were not*. Web page designers didn't claim to *program* Web pages; rather, they said that they *wrote*, *designed*, or *created* Web pages. You may wonder what the difference is. Programming is the process of developing a set of instructions that perform a specific function. Writing, designing, and creating are activities that communicate ideas. When executed, programs actively do things, whereas Web pages communicate ideas (by bringing together different media).

One type of media, interactive programs, did not exist in Web pages until the programming languages *Java* and *JavaScript* were made available. Now, besides communicating ideas, Web pages can also interactively do things as well. They add functionality to Web pages just as helpers and plug-ins do, but they provide much greater flexibility. The fundamental difference between the two languages is that *JavaScript* is usually integrated with the Web page and runs on the client side, whereas *Java* is usually integrated on the server side. The results are probably best understood by examining a few *Java* and *JavaScript* programs for yourself. If you are using Netscape *Navigator 2.0* or greater (or Microsoft *Internet Explorer 3.0* or greater), then you have the ability to view and interact with these programs.

The first three URLs will connect you to some really interesting examples of *Java*.

The Impressionist
   http://reality.sgi.com/employees/paul_asd/impression/index.html

Crossword Puzzle
   http://home.netscape.com/comprod/products/navigator/version_2.0/java_applets/Crossword

Conventional Wisdom
   http://www.pair.xerox.com/cw/

JavaChat
   http://members.aol.com/Nomo999/nomo7.htm

Java Applets
   http://www.javasoft.com:80/applets/

This last URL will connect you to a rather large collection of both *Java* and *JavaScript* examples.

   Depending on your system, these examples may take a while to load, so be patient.

Activity:
A Talkabout Tour

Learning doesn't stop when you leave the classroom or laboratory. The people around you, textbooks, libraries, and the Internet are all important resources that broaden your education. In particular, the Web, newsgroups, chat rooms, and e-mail can all help you become well-rounded and well-connected.

E-mail
Because you have a wealth of information at your fingertips, take the time to get some e-mail addresses from your instructor or other students. Most good e-mail software will provide you with a mechanism to store these addresses for easy retrieval. Begin exchanging e-mail with some of these people and you'll find that there is plenty of help available when you need it.

Newsgroups
Make it a practice to browse newsgroups. Plenty are of general interest; you should also make a habit of checking into a newsgroup that focuses on important topics discussed in class. By visiting many different newsgroups, you'll always have the latest scoop in a variety of subjects.

Chat
Chat rooms may or may not enhance your education. However, you might be able to find a chat room that is relatively empty. If so, arrange a fixed weekly time when you and your classmates can get together to work out problems or discuss material covered that week. A better option is to meet in person, but if this is impossible, chat rooms can provide an alternative.

Web Page
If you are using an ISP for Internet access, then you probably have access to posting information on your homepage. Consider using it as a way to bring other students together for discussion. Check with your instructor and you may find that he or she is willing to help you with this activity.

Chapter 4
Back to the Future
Advanced Techniques

The medium is the message.

No matter how enjoyable and interesting traveling is, it's always good to come home. Traveling in cyberspace is a little bit like traveling through time. It's very easy to lose several hours in what appears to be just a few ticks of the clock. Jet lag is uncomfortable, but virtual time lag may be even more unsettling: All the more reason to have a home in cyberspace to unwind your clock. This chapter will help you design a homepage on the Web and introduce you to setting up a Web server.

To gain the most from this chapter, you will need a few basic skills. You should be capable of creating, moving, and renaming directories and files on your computer. Also, you should be able to install applications onto your computer and set them up to function properly. With these skills, you should be able to follow the concepts outlined in the rest of this chapter. Keep in mind that what follows is not a step-by-step description of Web page design or Web server maintenance, but only an introduction to some basic concepts. You may want to supplement this discussion by consulting additional resources.

Section 4.1
There's no place like home—Designing

The following description will help you create your own homepage. It is not as simple as cruising the Web, but it's not hard either. Web pages are stored on a Web server. However, you can create a file on your home computer or a floppy disk that will act as a homepage. Ultimately, you will need access to a Web server to make your homepage part of the Internet. If your campus has a Web server, it may provide a place for student homepages. If you are using an ISP, you will probably be able to post a homepage at no additional cost. For the moment, though, let's focus on building a homepage even if you decide not to post it.

Homepages

What good is a homepage? You will find many uses; just a few are mentioned here. A homepage can be used to organize important and frequently-accessed links and bookmarks to the Internet, keeping you connected to a variety of resources from around over the world. It's better than a library card.

A homepage can also help you follow personal interests. For example, you can keep links to online magazines, the weather at your favorite camping spots, movie, music, and book reviews, newsgroups, the current news reports, pages with online games, your school's homepage, your friends' pages, the manuals for your e-mail and Web browsers, and your favorite search engines and directories. Some homepages reflect the personality of the owner who may post information about herself or himself for others to view.

Or imagine designing a homepage and turning it in as homework. You could turn in an assignment with online data, animations, video clips, and sound. You could have graphs that link directly to the data, pictures in color with an audio caption, interactive diagrams to illustrate your point, and an e-mail link if the instructor wanted to ask you a question. Move over, word-processor!

Now, where is your homepage?!? If you look at Appendix I, you'll see a template for a homepage. It is written in *HTML*, a simple language that Web browsers use to read hypertext documents. The initials stand for *HyperText Markup Language*. Right now, you might want to glance at it just to see what HTML looks like. Later on, you will be able to use this template and customize it as much as you like.

To get an idea of what homepages are like, use the following URLs to see what others have done. Some of these may appeal to you while others may not—homepage design is a personal choice.

Make A Friend On The *Web*
http://albrecht.ecn.purdue.edu/~jbradfor/homepage/

The People Page
http://www.peoplepage.com/

Laws of Cool Page
http://humanitas.ucsb.edu/shuttle/cool.html

Just as with cars, you can go manual or automatic when you design a web page. Both methods have advantages and disadvantages. When you design a page manually, you actually write with HTML (like shifting gears for the car). You'll have to learn some rather obscure notations but you will be able to fully control the look and feel of the page you create. Because most people want to design a page easily, tools have been developed to automate the process. These tools are called WYSIWYG (pronounced wizzy-wig) editors. (WYSIWYG stands for What You See Is What You Get.) The disadvantage of WYSIWYG tools is that you have less control over page design; the advantage is that you can save a considerable amount of time. Many designers use WYSIWYG tools for their initial layout and then tweak the HTML code to get what they want. Here is a little bit about each method. It should be enough to get you started.

Automatic

You can use several tools for WYSIWYG design. Some of them let you view the HTML as you design your page; in others, the code is hidden. We will focus on Netscape's WYSIWYG tool which is called *Navigator Gold*. Basically, it consists of *Navigator* with a built-in editor. (We'll refer to these two parts as the Browser and the Editor.) This software is free to both students and educators and you can get it directly from Netscape. Before you read on, download *Navigator Gold* 3.0 from Netscape's download site and install it on your computer. The address of the site is

http://home.netscape.com/comprod/products/navigator/gold/index.html

---

Choice is a great thing. Instead of relying solely on the information people give you, check for yourself, too. You may turn up something better that meets your needs. Here are a few more WYSIWYG editors for you to evaluate.

Microsoft FrontPage
 http://www.microsoft.com/frontpage/

HotMetal Pro
 http://www.sq.com/products/hotmetal/hmp-org.htm

HotDog Pro
 http://www.sausage.com/

Investigate the numerous WYSIWYG editors on the market carefully. Henry Ford said that when you bought a Model A, you could have any color you wanted as long as it was black. It's the same with some WYSIWYG editors.

Now we're ready to get started. You should have installed Netscape *Navigator Gold* 3.0. If you select *Options* from the menu bar, you will see an additional preference command titled *Editor Preferences*.... Select this and a window will appear (Figure 4.1). Three tabs are found at the top of this preference window. Select the *General* tab and enter your name (as you will soon be an author). You should also enter information for your preferred HTML text editor and image editor.

Are you wondering why you need another HTML editor? Keep in mind that WYSIWYG editors are not the end-all and be-all of document creation. Occasionally you'll want some manual control over both the pages and the images you embed in them. But you don't need to buy any more software. All you need is a simple text editor, which is probably included with your computer. If you are using a Macintosh operating system, you can use either *TeachText* or *SimpleText*. If you are using a Windows-based operating system, you can use either *Notepad* or *Wordpad*. Use the *Browse...* button to locate the text editor you'd like to use.

The image editor may not be included with your operating system. However, you don't need one to follow our discussion. When you need one later on, check on the Internet, where numerous image editors are available for free. Use your search engine to locate an image editor.

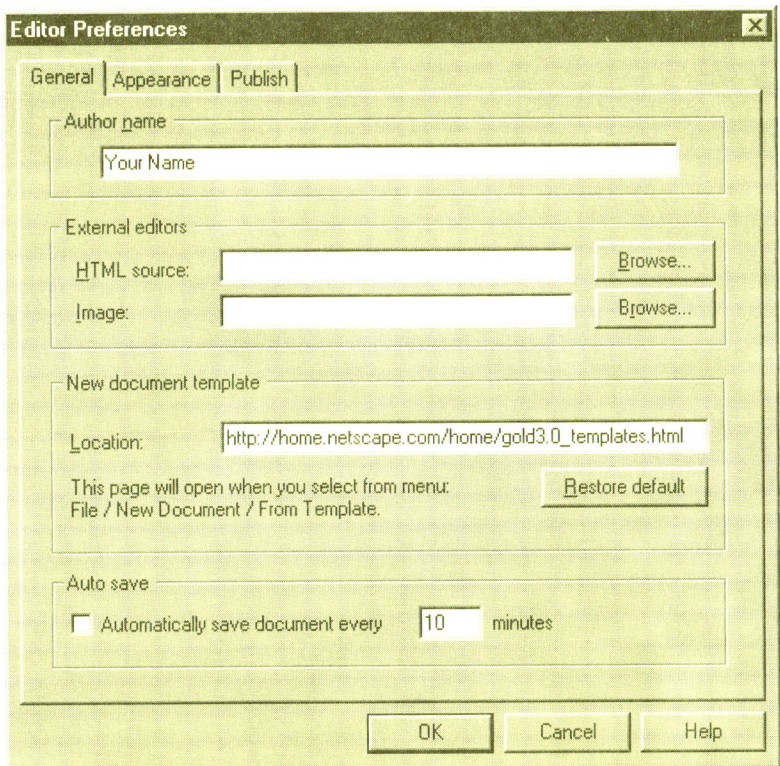

Figure 4.1. Opening the *Editor Preferences* selection in *Navigator Gold* will activate this window.

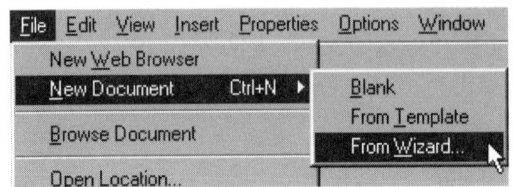

Figure 4.2. Opening *Netscape's Page Wizard* is accessible from the menu bar on *Navigator Gold*.

The next section in the *General* tab is where you enter the URL for a page template source. Don't worry about it now. Select the OK button and your settings will be saved.

Templates

Netscape has organized a wonderful little resource to help first time Web authors write their first page quickly and easily. This is done online and all you need to do is follow along. In no time, you'll have a simple homepage.

To get started, select File from the menu bar and choose *New Document* and then choose *From Wizard...*(Figure 4.2). You may also use the following URL:

http://home.netscape.com/home/gold3.0_wizard.html

The *Page Wizard* (Figure 4.3) is divided into three unique windows (or frames). Read the basic instructions from the upper right window and select START when you are ready.

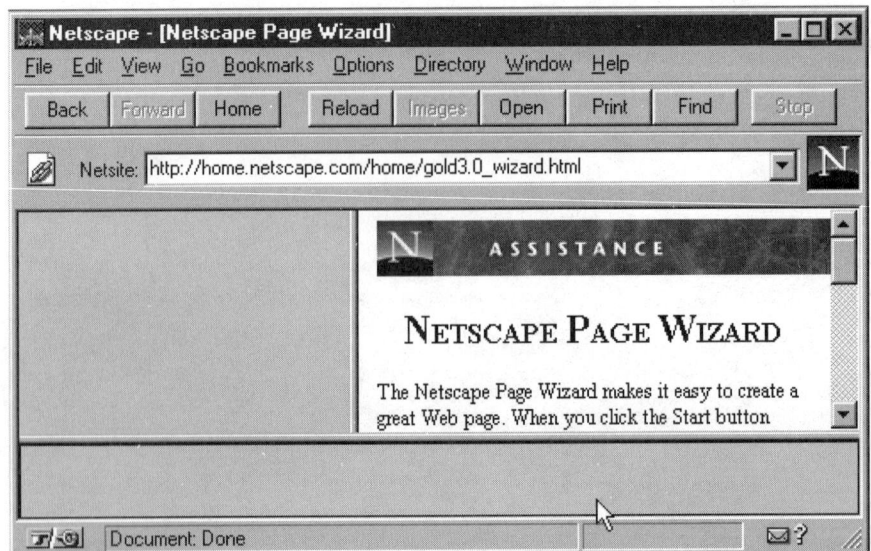

Figure 4.3. Netscape's Page Wizard is available only online and you will need to have an Internet connection to use it.

Once you've started, you'll see a set of instructions in the upper left window. Although the instructions are self-explanatory, here's a brief overview of what you need to do. You'll be working in a counter-clockwise direction.

1. Read the instructions in the left window.
2. Click each hyperlink as you come to it in the instructions.
3. Enter the requested information in the lower window.
4. View the information as it appears in the right window.
5. Modify the information (lower window) until you like what you see.
6. Continue executing the instructions until you get to the end.

When you've executed all of the instructions, select the *Build* button and your first homepage will be displayed in the Browser window.

What have you accomplished so far? Basically, you've used a remote tool (Netscape's *Page Wizard*) to create a homepage from a preset template. Everything that you are now looking at is still on Netscape's server and not your computer. You can't do anything more to your homepage until you move it over to your machine.

Select the *Edit* button from the tool bar at the top of the Browser. (If you aren't using the *Gold* version, you will need to download it from Netscape—it's free.) An Editor window (Figure 4.4) will open along with a dialog box asking if you wish to bring over the associated images and preserve the links, which *you do*. You will then get a dialog window to determine the location on your computer where you wish to save the file and images. If you expect to do a lot of Web page design, you should create a directory where you can store all of your pages.

Unlike documents that you may have made with a word processor, Web documents don't combine all of their elements into one package. The text,

Figure 4.4. The *Editor* window is significantly different from that of the *Browser*

which consists of words and code, is in a file that has an *.htm* or *.html* suffix. All of the associated elements—which may include images, sounds, and other non-text information—are in separate files with suffixes such as *.gif*, *.jpe*, and others. Navigator Gold brings all of these pieces together when you save a page to your computer.

WYSIWYG

At this point, you still haven't used the Editor portion of *Navigator Gold*. Now that you've saved your new homepage to your local machine, you are ready to add any desired text using the Editor.

Let's review the work you've completed so far. With Netscape *Navigator Gold* installed, you used the *Page Wizard* and generated a simple homepage from a template. You downloaded that page to your server and then you opened it in the Editor portion of *Navigator Gold*. There are also other templates available at the Netscape site. You can save them or any other page in this same way. (Note, however, that some pages you'll find on the Web contain copyrighted information.)

Next, let's do a couple of things so you can see how easy it is to use the Editor. Then you can experiment with the software to explore all your options. Later on you might want to check out your library (or local bookstore) to learn more about designing Web pages. You'll find a great selection of books that will help you to understand all of the details of *Navigator Gold* or any other WYSIWYG editor.

To familiarize yourself with the Editor, move your cursor over the top of each Editor button and pause (but don't click the mouse button) until the label appears. Reading the labels should help you discover the function of each button.

Remember to always save your original page! This means that after you've done something cool to your page, save it as a different file. By doing so, you can always retrieve the last page if you realize that your change wasn't really as great as you first thought.

Here are a couple of things to do to your homepage that will start you on your way:

1. Modify (size, color, style, etc.) the text on your page.
2. Enter a new paragraph of text.
3. Enter a bulleted list of information.
4. Place a horizontal line.
5. Insert an image.
6. Embed a link to an e-mail address.
7. Embed a link to an URL on the Web.

8. Create a new document and then embed a link from your homepage to this new document.

Here are two great sites to help you learn more about designing a Web page. You'll find images, icons, backgrounds, and a lot of guidance.

Netscape Gold Authoring Guide
http://home.netscape.com/eng/mozilla/3.0/handbook/authoring/navgold.htm

Netscape's Gold Rush Tool Chest
http://home.netscape.com/assist/net_sites/starter/samples/index.html

Hint: To capture an image you need only to be able to see it. For Macintosh users, click on the image and just hold down a second longer than you normally would. A window will appear with save options. For *Windows*, use the right mouse button and you'll get the same options window.

Now you have a homepage! Right? Well, don't worry if it still isn't perfect. You have plenty of time to make it shine. Or you may be perfectly satisfied with what you created using the Editor. If so, you may want to read the next section later; we will explain a little bit about how to take the manual design approach by using HTML. The extra effort may be very worthwhile if you plan to create Web sites that are more complex.

Take a look at the HTML code of the page you just created. While you have the Editor window active, select *View* from the menu bar and then select *Edit Document Source* (Figure 4.5). This will open the text editor you designated in the *Editor Preferences* and display the HTML code for your page.

You may want to print a copy of the HTML code in your homepage. Unless you got carried away with the Editor, this will allow you to see your homepage on one or two sheets.

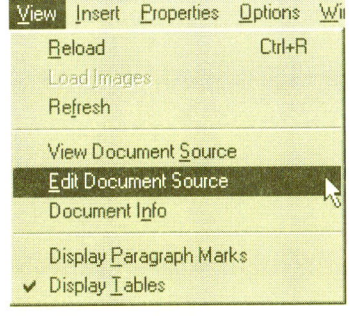

Figure 4.5. This pull-down menu is available only while the Editor portion of *Navigator Gold* is active. *View Document Source* will display the source but will not allow you to modify it. *Edit Document Source* will allow you to modify the HTML code.

Manual

The HTML code on your homepage is really pretty easy to understand. You need to remember only a couple of things in order to read HTML. For the moment, ignore the HTML and focus on the rest of the document—you'll see that it makes sense. You can do this by alternately viewing your homepage file through Navigator and then through your text editor. You don't need a fancy program to write or edit HTML, just a text editor and a basic understanding of the code.

Now, look at the window with the HTML code. At the very top you'll see a tag like this: <HTML>. A *tag* is an element of HTML code. It is added to the page to emphasize the text that will appear on the viewed Web page. Tags always have an angle bracket (<) followed by one or more letters and a reverse angle bracket (>). Here are some examples: <BODY>, <HEAD>, and <TITLE>.

Most HTML tags come in pairs. For example, the tag <HEAD>, found on the second line of the program, is accompanied by a corresponding tag </HEAD> (see the fourth line). The second member of each tag pair has a forward slash (/) preceding the word. The other members of tag pairs are </BODY> and </TITLE>. Tags, when used in sets or pairs, surround a section of text and define the beginning and end of an HTML section. It is possible to use tags incorrectly just as it is possible to use English incorrectly. Here is an example of a properly-coded HTML page:

<HTML>
   <HEAD>
      This is where a description and purpose of the page is written. The material is not viewed on the browser. It is only used to document the intent of the page.
   </HEAD>
   <BODY>
      This is where the material that is to be viewed through the browser will be written.
   </BODY>
</HTML>

All properly-coded HTML documents have this basic format. Notice the beginning and ending member of each tag pair. Although tags usually operate in pairs, some are used as solitary tags. When you want to separate sections of text with two spaces, you could use the paragraph tag, <P>. Two line break tags, <BR>, will also do the same thing. If you want the browser to make a horizontal line across the viewed page, then you use a horizontal line tag, <HR>. You may have noticed that the tag names are abbreviations of what they do. You don't have to learn everything about HTML now, however. You can embed some of these features with your WYSIWYG editor.

> If you really want to jump into HTML, here are a few Web sites that may be helpful to you.
>
> **Netscape Page Starter Site**
> http://home.netscape.com/home/starter.html
>
> **Webreference**
> http://www.webreference.com/
>
> **HTML Hot Tips**
> http://members.aol.com/htmlguru/tips/

Other people have already created enticing homepages and you might want to use theirs as a template if you don't like yours or the one in Appendix I. Simply find the interesting pages that other people have developed, copy the code and modify it to reflect your own personality or interests.

Hyperlinks

One very important element in HTML is the code for hyperlinks (jumping points within Web pages). You know most of what you need to know to create hyperlinks. The HTML tag pair for a hyperlink is <A> and </A>. There are two main components to a link. The first element is the URL of the document to which the link leads and the second is the word (or words) to be set as a hyperlink. You can also enter links into your pages with the Editor. Here is an example of how to write a link tag:

    <A HREF="URL">
       Word
    </A>

This may seem a little complicated but it's not difficult. The first line of the example above begins the code for a link. The letters and signs between the angle brackets represent an URL which tells the browser the location of the requested document. The second line is the hypertext link that will appear in color on the Web page. The link tag pair is completed with the ending link tag, </A>. When on an actual Web page, the hypertext link can be selected by a user who will be sent to the page specified by the URL.

> In this exercise, use your text editor and type in the basic page elements discussed earlier (<HTML> and </HTML>). Within the body of the page, type in a link tag pair using a real URL. Use one or all of the examples provided below. Once you have this page, save it with the name TEST.HTML and view it with your browser. (You do not have to be online for any of this.)
>
> **A Beginner's Guide to HTML**
> http://www.ncsa.uiuc.edu/General/Internet/WWW/HTMLPrimer.html
>
> **How to Publish on the Web**
> http://www.thegiim.org/
>
> **The Bare Bones Guide to HTML**
> http://werbach.com/barebones/
>
> See step 2 in the section below for help in finding and displaying the file. Once you've got this page up and running on your browser, try the hyperlink online. Does it work? These URLs should take you to resources that will tell you more about Web publishing.

Home

You now have a homepage. Where do you put it to make it work? This depends on whether you will have access to a Web server or not. The instructions that follow assume that you don't have access. Once you've completed your homepage, you'll have a file on either your hard drive or a floppy disk. The advantage of having your homepage on floppy disk is that you'll have a portable homepage that you can use on any computer. Here is a five-step procedure for finding and setting your default homepage to the one you've created.

1. *After* you finished the end-of-chapter activity, you should copy your intended homepage to either a floppy disk or your hard drive.
2. With *Navigator*, you should be able to find a command under the *File* menu called *Open* File.... If you initiate this command, you'll get a dialog window where you can designate the file you wish to open. You want to open your homepage which at the moment is not on a server. Select the HTML file for your homepage from either your floppy disk or hard drive and press the *Return* key. Your browser will open your homepage and display it for you.
3. If it isn't set already, change your *Options* setting so you can view the URLs of the pages that are displayed on your browser. When this is set properly, you'll notice that your file's URL is listed something like this: file:/// . . . ./file.html. The protocol is no longer HTTP and there are more than two slashes.

4. Record this URL on a piece of paper so that you can refer to it in the next step. (Every slash and colon is significant.)
5. Earlier in this chapter, we discussed how to change the homepage designation for your browser. First, open the *General Preferences* section of the *Options* menu. Then select the *General* tab and enter the URL that you wrote down in step 4 into the homepage entry window.

Now that you've performed these steps, your browser should automatically jump to your homepage when you select the *Home* button from the toolbar. Try it. The procedures that you've just performed have allowed your browser to memorize the location of your homepage file. If you move it or erase it, you'll have to do this *all* over again.

The Future

If you want to learn more about tags, it's not hard to do so. Various places on the Web offer online tutorials on HTML design. Links to some of these places are found in the homepage template provided in Appendix I. As you learn more about the Internet and HTML, you'll discover ways to manually add pictures to your pages. Later you'll even begin adding sounds and maybe a video clip or two. The tools available to you today barely hint at what will be available to you in the future.

Section 4.2
Opening your own shop—Serving

A few of you may want to assemble and maintain an active Web server. If so, you'll need an extra measure of determination. A Web server is not necessarily easy to manage; you'll need to develop skills beyond those required to cruise the Net. However, doing so is well within your ability if you know how to get help and find resources. This enterprise will require a considerable amount of time, equipment, and money, but it will give you more control.

The Shopping List
To set up a server on the Web, you need four basic components:

Computer
Software
Internet Connection
A Willing Participant

It's the last element of the list that stops most people. If you are going to set up a server, then you need someone who is willing *and* able to spend a considerable amount of time maintaining and managing it. If this someone is you, make sure you have the time and energy for it.

Because of the many tasks it must perform, the computer server should be dedicated to that purpose alone. The following list contains suggestions for a basic server.

Hardware:
    Pentium computer
    36 MB RAM
    2 GB Hard Drive
    CD-ROM Drive
    Network Interface Card
    Keyboard and Monitor

Software:
    Server Operating System
    Web Server Software
    Mail and News Server Software (Optional)

Connection:
    ISDN or T1

We suggest a *Pentium* because they are relatively cheap and common. You don't need a really fast system like a *Pentium Pro* because a server typically doesn't need speed, just the bandwidth for the Internet connection. A *Pentium* also offers the flexibility of serving files to both *Macintosh* computers and PCs.

System memory is important if you want to run multiple elements like a mail server and a news server. The same goes for the hard drive. You'll need some storage but keep in mind that you can always add to your system later on: Hard drives continue to get cheaper, faster, and larger. If you don't need extra memory and storage now, then wait and save your money. The CD-ROM is probably essential if you have to do any software installation. Without it, you'll quickly learn how time consuming it can be to install software for one program using, say, 50 floppy disks. The network interface card is used to connect your computer to your network (campus or outside provider). Take your provider's suggestions when purchasing the network card. The monitor (and keyboard) need not be expensive because you won't be doing any fancy graphic work.

For the software we suggest *Windows NT 4.0 Server* as the base operating system: It is cheap, powerful, easy to use, growing in popularity (this means you'll be able to get lots of help), and can handle a mix of both *Macintosh* computers and PCs. A great deal of software is currently being developed for *Windows NT*, so you won't have a difficult time finding compatible application programs.

For Web server software, Microsoft *Internet Information Server (IIS)* is included free with the *Windows NT*. Netscape also provides Web server software for *Windows NT*. It, too, is free. The *IIS* software may be slightly more intuitive to use, but you may find otherwise. Try them both. If you're interested in setting up a mail or news server, you will need additional software. These come in separate packages and are also commonly available from both Microsoft and Netscape. Our advice is to start with a Web server and add more when you're comfortable with what you've created.

The components of a Web server are less expensive than in the past but the computer and software will probably cost about $5000 in today's market. However, hardware and software are not your only expenses. A Web server without a network connection is nearly useless. Even if you want to set up an internal network (Intranet), you'll need the basic wires and connections to other computers. Keep in mind that your school may be able to make a Web server possible by providing computer resources that would otherwise be too expensive to purchase. If your school cannot offer such assistance, you will have to rent Internet access on a monthly basis. This will probably cost a considerable amount of money. Thus, be sure that you have a compelling need for a server before you begin to assemble one.

If you do put together a server, you may need additional equipment to ensure its security such as a tape backup system and an uninterruptible power supply (UPS). If your information is really valuable, you may want to even consider locking everything in a back room with a redundant server.

If you're determined to build a Web server, the following Web sites describe how to set up, maintain, and administer a Windows NT server. You'll also be able to download free versions of Web server software from Microsoft, Netscape, and other companies.

Web66 Windows NT Cookbook
http://web66.coled.umn.edu/WinNT/CookBook/Default.html

Netscape's Education Program
http://home.netscape.com/comprod/server_central/edu_drive.html

Microsoft's Education Program
http://www.microsoft.com/education/hed/default.htm

Activity:
Show that You've Arrived

If you've been reading this chapter with your hands on a computer keyboard, then you're close to having a homepage of your own. This final activity is designed to take you the rest of the way. Using the template provided in Appendix I, you will be able to build a homepage that you can keep on a floppy disk.

We use several different fonts to distinguish various elements of the homepage template in Appendix I. *Large italic font* is used to represent the text that you are to replace with your information. HTML tags are represented in a <SMALLER FONT, ALL IN UPPER-CASE AND WITH ANGLE BRACKETS>. Text that is not an HTML tag and does not need to be changed is in a regular size and font.

Take the time now to add some flash to whatever template you choose. After you have completed entering your information, save your work (either to a floppy or hard disk) using a file name, such as HOMENAME, with an HTML suffix (that is, save the file as HOMENAME.HTML). You can use the file on your home computer or you can post it on your campus Web server or your ISP.

If you choose to post your homepage on your campus Web server or with your ISP, register your site at **http://www.liquidimaging.com/liqimg/submit/submit.html** to make sure your homepage is listed in the Web directories and search engines. With world-wide exposure, you will have indeed arrived. See you on the Web!

Appendix I
Stepping Out
Student Homepage Template

In the electric age we wear all mankind as our skin.

```
<HTML>
<HEAD>
      <TITLE>Your Homepage</TITLE>
</HEAD>

<BODY>
<CENTER>
      <H1>Your Name</H1>
      <H2>Your Title, Major, or Philosophy of Life</H2>
      <H3>
      <ADDRESS>
            Your address<BR>
            May<BR>
            Go<BR>
            Here<BR>
            <P>
            Your e-mail address<BR>
      </ADDRESS>
      </H3>
</CENTER>
<HR>

<DL>
      <H2>This Is Your Life:</H2>
      <DD>Just say something about yourself. After you've added some
            information to your homepage file, compare it to what actually shows
```

on your browser. You'll notice that most of the HTML code is not visible.

    \<P\>

    \<DD\>*You can have as many paragraphs as you wish. Here's another paragraph.*

    \<P\>

\</DL\>

\<DL\>

    \<H2\>*Important Resources*\</H2\>

    \<DD\>

        \<A HREF="http://www.ssnewslink.com"\>

        NewsLink from Simon and Schuster

        \</A\>

\</DL\>

\<HR\>

\<DL\>

    \<H2\>Handbooks and Manuals\</H2\>

    \<DD\>

        \<A HREF="http://www.matisse.net/files/glossary.html"\>

        Glossary of Internet Terms

        \</A\>

    \<DD\>

        \<A HREF="http://home.netscape.com/eng/mozilla/3.0/handbook/"\>

        Netscape Handbook

        \</A\>

    \<DD\>

        \<A HREF="http://home.netscape.com/eng/mozilla/3.0/handbook/authoring/navgold.htm"\>

        Netscape Gold Authoring Guide

        \</A\>

\</DL\>

\<HR\>

\<DL\>

    \<H2\>Directories and Search Engines: \</H2\>

    \<DD\>

        \<A HREF="http://www.lycos.com"\>

        Lycos Search Engine

        \</A\>

    \<DD\>

        \<A HREF="http://www.Webcrawler.*com*/"\>

        WebCrawler Search Engine

        \</A\>

```
        <DD>
                <A HREF="http://www.yahoo.com/">
                        Yahoo Directory
                </A>
</DL>
<HR>
<DL>
        <H2>Design and Publish: </H2>
        <DD>
                <A HREF="http://www.ncsa.uiuc.edu/General/Internet/WWW/HTMLPrimer.html">
                        A Beginner's Guide to HTML
                </A>
        <DD>
                <A HREF="http://werbach.com/barebones/">
                        The BareBones Guide to HTML
                </A>
        <DD>
                <A HREF="http://www.thegiim.org/">
                        How to Publish On The Web
                </A>
        <DD>
                <A HREF="http://home.netscape.com/assist/net_sites/starter/samples/index.html">
                        Netscape's Gold Rush Tool Chest
                </A>
</DL>
<HR>
<H3>
        Your Name <A HREF="mailto:Name@server.edu">e-mail address<\A>
</H3>

</BODY>
</HTML>
```

Appendix II
Internet Resources for Political Science

A hot medium is one that extends the single sense in "high definition." High definition is the state of being filled with data.

Here are a number of links that you should find "ve-e-ry interesting." Think of this as a starter kit for further investigation. We include websites for using the Internet, digital library websites, and general websites for the Humanities and Social Sciences. We then provide sites for Political Science.

    Several comments are in order before you begin surfing. First, don't be discouraged if your first try to link to a site produces a message like "Unable to connect to remote host." The rule of thumb is to try the same site three times in a row before proceeding to another URL. (Remember, you're still trying to communicate with the World Wide Wait.) Second, be careful typing site locations. If you mistype one character (capital letters matter), the address won't work. Third, Web sites come and go more often than print media. What is on the Internet today may be gone tomorrow. Fourth, a tilde (~) usually designates a site maintained by a person, rather than an organization or some "non-person." These are the sites most likely to disappear on the Web. Finally, we list just a few newsgroups. If you are interested in political history (or anyone who has done some research), there are more newsgroups than you could possibly dream of exploring. Try **http://www.tile.net/tile/news/** to unearth your favorite newsgroup. Get down!

Websites for Using the Internet

Internet Starter Kit (Macmillan Computer Publishing)
http://www.mcp.com/resources/geninternet

Web Resources
http://www.w3.org/

World Wide Web FAQ
http://sunsite.unc.edu/boutell/faq/faq.txt

Learn the Net
http://www.learnthenet.com/english/index.html

Understanding and Using the Internet
http://www2.pbs.org/uti/

Newbie Training
http://www.newbie.net/CyberCourse

The Internet for Social Scientists
http://www.unesco.org/most/brochur3.htm

Interactive Guide to the Internet
http://www.sierramm.com/smpnet.html

Digital Library Websites

Gateway to Europe's National Libraries
http://portico.bl.uk/gabriel/

Worldwide Digital Library Research Projects
http://www.dlib.org/projects.html#national

Digital Library Initiative (Social Science Team)
http://anshar.grainger.uiuc.edu/dlisoc/socsci_site/index.html

University of California at Berkeley
http://elib.cs.berkeley.edu/

University of Michigan
http://www.si.umich.edu/UMDL

University of Illinois
http://dli.grainger.uiuc.edu/

University of California at Santa Barbara
http://alexandria.sdc.ucsb.edu/

Carnegie Mellon University
http://www.informedia.cs.cmu.edu

Library of Congress Digital Library
http://www.loc.gov/

Berkeley Digital Library SunSITE
http://sunsite.berkeley.edu/

Humanities Texts
http://english-server.hss.cmu.edu

eLib Homepage
http://ukoln.bath.ac.uk/services/eLib/

The Electric Library
http://www.elibrary.com/

The Electric Newsstand
http://www.enews.com/

General Websites for Humanities and Social Sciences

The HUMBUL Gateway: International Resources for the Humanities
http://users.ox.ac.uk/~humbul/

Humanities HUB: Selected Resources for the Social Sciences
and Humanities
http://www.gu.edu.au/gwis/hub

Social Sciences Server
http://coombs.anu.edu.au/

INFOMINE for the Social Sciences, Humanities, and the Arts.
http://lib-www.ucr.edu/liberal/

The Argus Clearinghouse: Arts and Humanities
Social Sciences and Social Issues
http://www.clearinghouse.net/index.html

The WWW Virtual Library
http://www.ulib.stanford.edu/overview.html

Voice of the Shuttle Guide to the Humanities and Social Sciences
http://humanitas.ucsb.edu/

H-Net: Humanities and Social Sciences Online Home Page
http://h-net.msu.edu/

Social Science Information Gateway
http://sosig.ac.uk/

Forum on Technology, Media and Society
http://www.tunisia.sdc.ucsb.edu/speed/

Trade Wave Galaxy: Humanities/Social Science Indices
http://www.eitnet.net

Social Sciences Indices
http://www.osu.edu/units/sociology/indices.htm

Political Science Websites

American Government and Politics Resources List
http://www.lsu.edu/guests/poli/public_html/ampols.html

John F. Kennedy School of Government
http://ksgwww.harvard.edu/

The Political Scientist's Guide to the Internet
http://www.trincoll.edu/~pols/guide/home.html

Political Science Resources on the Web
http://www.lib.umich.edu/libhome/Documents.center/frames/polscifr.html

Political Science/Law
http://www.lib.lsu.edu/soc/pslaw.html

American Political Science Association
http://www.apsanet.org/

Political Science Virtual Library
http://www.lib.umich.edu/libhome/Documents.center/frames/polscifr.html

Political Science Resources
http://www.keele.ac.uk/depts/po/psr.htm

U.S. Federal Government Agencies Page
http://www.lib.lsu.edu/gov/fedgov.html

An Introduction to the U.S. Government
http://www.vote-smart.org/reference/primer/contents.html

The Great American Website
http://www.uncle-sam.com/unclesam/

The Federal Web Locator
http://www.law.vill.edu/Fed-Agency/fedwebloc.html

WWW U.S. Government Information Sources
http://www.nttc.edu/gov_res.html

United Nations
http://www.un.org/

U.S. Tax Code Online
http://www.fourmilab.ch/ustax/ustax.html

Office of Management and Budget
http://www.whitehouse.gov/WH/EOP/OMB/html/ombhome.html

Thomas
http://thomas.loc.gov/

U.S. House of Representatives
http://www.house.gov/

United States Senate
http://www.senate.gov/

Internal Revenue Service
http://www.irs.ustreas.gov/prod/

Federal Election Commission
http://www.fec.gov/

National Performance Review
http://www.npr.gov/

FedStats
http://www.fedstats.gov/

Federal World Search
http://www.fedworld.gov/

National Civic League
http://www.ncl.org/ncl/index.htm

State and Local Government on the Net
http://www.piperinfo.com/state/states.html

State and Local Governments
http://lcweb.loc.gov/global/state/stategov.html

State-based Think Tanks
http://www.cascadepolicy.org/spn.htm

The Council of State Governments
http://www.csg.org/

Full-text State Statutes and Legislation on the Internet
http://www.prairienet.org/~scruffy/f.htm

State Bar Associations
http://www.martindale.com/profession/state_bars.html

National Conference of State Legislatures
http://www.ncsl.org/

National Governors' Association
http://www.nga.org/

National Association of State Budget Officers
http://www.nasbo.org/

State Tax Resources
http://omer.actg.uic.edu/othersites/stateinfo.html

County and City Data Books
http://www.lib.virginia.edu/socsci/ccdb/

Census of Governments
http://www.census.gov/govs/www/govstruc.html

Finance Net
http://www.financenet.gov/

Federalist Papers
http://www.law.uoknor.edu/hist/federalist/

The Jefferson Project
http://www.voxpop.org/jefferson/

Constitution Society
http://www.constitution.org/

U.S. Constitution
http://www.law.cornell.edu/constitution/constitution.overview.html

James Madison
http://www.jmu.edu/polisci/madison/madison.htm

Documents from the Continental Congress
http://rs6.loc.gov/ammem/bdsds/bdsdhome.html

Colonial USA
http://www.msstate.edu/Archives/History/USA/colonial/colonial.html

U.S. Historical Documents
http://kuhttp.cc.ukans.edu/carrie/docs/docs_us.html

Madison's Notes
http://teaminfinity.com/madison.html

Supreme Court Decisions
http://supct.law.cornell.edu/supct/

American Bar Association
http://www.abanet.org/

CourtTV
http://www.courttv.com/index.html#Top

FindLaw
http://www.findlaw.com/

Touro Law Center
http://www.tourolaw.edu/

The U.S. House of Representatives Internet Law Library
http://law.house.gov/1.htm

World Wide Web Virtual Library: Law: Main Index
http://www.law.indiana.edu/law/v-lib/lawindex.html

Glossary of Legal Terms
http://www.id.uscourts.gov/glossary.htm

CIESIN
http://www.ciesin.org/

American Demographics
http://www.demographics.com/

Whitehouse
http://www2.whitehouse.gov/WH/Welcome.html

American Voter
http://voter96.cqalert.com/

Political Chat
http://www.4-lane.com/politicalchat/

All Things Political
http://dolphin.gulf.net/Political.html

CongressOrg
http://207.168.215.81/

Census Bureau
http://www.census.gov/

Statistical Abstract of the United States
http://www.census.gov/statab/www/

Social Statistics Briefing Room (SSBR)
http://www2.whitehouse.gov/fsbr/ssbr.html

Project Vote Smart
http://www.vote-smart.org/

Campaign Finance Reform
http://www.brookings.org/GS/campaign/home.htm

Center for Voting and Democracy
http://open.igc.org/cvd/

Election Calendar
http://www.ifes.org/eleccal.htm

League of Women Voters
http://www.main.org/leaguewv/home.html

Votelink
http://www.votelink.com

National Election Studies (NES)
http://www.umich.edu/~nes/

The U.S. Electoral College Calculator
http://www.bga.com/~jnhtx/ec/ec.html

World Elections
http://www.psr.keele.ac.uk/election.htm

Center for Responsive Politics
http://www.crp.org/index.html-ssi

Political Science Resources Think Tanks
http://www.lib.umich.edu/libhome/Documents.center/psthink.html

Electronic Policy Network
http://epn.org/

Policy.Com
http://policy.com/

Centers for Research and Policy Development
http://ksgwww.harvard.edu/~library/resorgs.htm

The American Communication Association
http://cavern.uark.edu/depts/comminfo/www/ACA.html

Common Cause
http://www.commoncause.org/

The National Rifle Association of America
http://www.nra.org/

MADD On-Line
http://www.madd.org/

PACronyms
http://www.crp.org/cgi-win/pacronym.exe

American Association of Retired People
http://www.aarp.org/

Government & Politics on the Net Project
http://www.sscf.ucsb.edu/~survey1/

Media Watch
http://theory.lcs.mit.edu/~mernst/media/

Magazine Search
http://www.stpt.com/magazine/magazine.html

U.S.News
http://www2.usnews.com/usnews/

The Atlantic Monthly
http://www.theatlantic.com/atlantic/

National Public Radio
http://www.npr.org/

U.S. Budget.Com
http://www.usbudget.com/

Center for Tax Justice
http://www.ctj.org/

Budget Simulator
http://garnet.berkeley.edu:3333/

Bureau of the Public Debt
http://www.publicdebt.treas.gov/

Frequently Requested Statistical Releases
http://www.stat-usa.gov/BEN/newsrel.html

Political Parties
http://www.agora.stm.it/politic/usa1.htm

Lighthouse List of Political Parties
http://www.sjca.edu/~cgillen/lighthouse.html

C-Span
http://www.c-span.org/

Liberalism Resurgent
http://www.scruz.net/~kangaroo/tenets.htm

Right Side of the Web
http://www.rtside.com/

Survey of American Political Culture
http://minerva.acc.virginia.edu/~postmod/Survey_Home.html

Online Survey Research/Public Opinion Centers: A Worldwide Listing
http://www.ukans.edu/cwis/units/coms2/po/index.html

Institute for Social Research
http://www.isr.umich.edu/

Public Opinion Links
http://www.smpcollege.com:80/smp_govt/opinion.htm

American Civil Liberties Union
http://www.aclu.org/

Oyez Oyez Oyez
http://court.it-services.nwu.edu/oyez/

The Center for Democracy and Technology
http://www.cdt.org/

NAACP Online
http://www.naacp.org/

Separation of Church and State Home Page
http://www.louisville.edu/~tnpete01/church/index.htm

Presidential Elections
http://www.multied.com/elections/index.html

Grolier's Online: The American Presidency
http://gi.grolier.com/presidents/preshome.html

Presidents of the United States
http://www.ipl.org/ref/POTUS/

Presidential Libraries IDEA Network
http://sunsite.unc.edu/lia/president/

Political Babble Generator
http://www.webcorp.com/polibabble.htm

Search Political Newgroups
http://www.intbc.com/sleuth/poli-n.html

History and Political Science Web Resources and Discussion Groups
http://ashland.edu/hispol.html

Science Newsgroups

alt.activism
alt.politics.clinton
alt.politics.media
alt.politics.equality
alt.politics.reform
alt.politics.elections
alt.politics.usa.republican
alt.politics.democrats
alt.politics.radical-left
alt.politics.libertarian
trial.talk.politics.peace
talk.politics.theory

Appendix III
Documenting Your Electronic Sources

Copyright laws came into effect when people started realizing that income could be made by selling their words. In an era dubbed "The Age of Information," knowledge and words are taking on more significance than ever. Laws requiring writers to *document* or give credit to the sources of their information, while evolving, are still in effect.

Various organizations have developed style manuals detailing, among other style matters, how to document sources in their particular disciplines. For writing in English composition and literature, Modern Language Association (MLA) and American Psychological Assocation (APA) guidelines are the most commonly used, but others such as those in *The Chicago Manual of Style* (CMS), are available. Always find out from your instructor what style to use in a specific assignment so that you can follow the appropriate guidelines.

For general information on MLA and APA citations, the best print sources are:

Gibaldi, Joseph. <u>MLA Handbook for Writers of Research Papers</u>. 4th ed. NY: MLA, 1995.

American Psychological Association. <u>Publication Manual of the American Psychological Association</u>. 4th ed. Washington: APA, 1994.

Because the methods of obtaining electronic information are developing so rapidly, printed style manuals have had difficulty in keeping up with the changes and in developing documentation styles for electronic sources. As a result, the most up-to-date information from the MLA and the APA about documenting online sources with URLs can be found on these organizations' Web sites. This Appendix shows you how to credit your electronic sources based on the information there.

When you cite electronic sources, it is vital to type every letter, number, symbol, and space accurately. Any error makes it impossible to retrieve your source. Since electronic sources tend to be transitory, printing a hard copy of your sources will make it easier for you to cite accurately and provide evidence for your documentation. MLA style encloses Internet addresses and URLs (Uniform Resource Locators) in angle brackets < >. If you see them around an address, do not use them as part of the address when you attempt to retrieve the source. APA style does not enclose URLs.

Modern Language Association (MLA) Style Guidelines

These guidelines follow the documentation style authorized by the Modern Language Association for electronic sources. Web sources are documented in basically the same way as traditional sources. According to the MLA Web site, the following items should be included if they are available:

1. Name of the author, editor, compiler, or translator of the source (if available and relevant), reversed for alphabetizing and followed by an abbreviation, such as *ed.*, if appropriate
2. Title of a poem, short story, article, or similar short work within a scholarly project, database, or periodical (in quotation marks); or title of a posting to a discussion list or forum (taken from the subject line and put in quotation marks), followed by the description *Online posting*
3. Title of a book (underlined)
4. Name of the editor, compiler, or translator of the text (if relevant and if not cited earlier), preceded by the appropriate abbreviation, such as *ed.*
5. Publication information for any print version of the source
6. Title of the scholarly project, database, periodical, or professional or personal site (underlined); or, for a professional or personal site with no title, a description such as *Home page*
7. Name of the editor of the scholarly project or database (if available)
8. Version number of the source (if not part of the title) or, for a journal, the volume number, issue number, or other identifying number
9. Date of electronic publication, of the latest update, or of posting
10. For a posting to a discussion list or forum, the name of the list or forum
11. The number range or total number of pages, paragraphs, or other sections, if they are numbered
12. Name of any institution or organization sponsoring or associated with the Web site

13. Date when the researcher accessed the source
14. Electronic address, or URL, of the source (in angle brackets)

From the Modern Language Association (MLA) <http://www.mla.org/main.stl.htm>.

Examples:

Book
Shaw, Bernard. <u>Pygmalion</u>. 1912. Bartleby Archive. 6 Mar. 1998 <http://www.columbia.edu/acis/bartleby/shaw/>.

Poem
Carroll, Lewis. "Jabberwocky." 1872. 6 Mar. 1998. <http://www.jabberwocky.com/carroll/jabber/jabberwocky.html>.

Article in a Journal
Rehberger, Dean. "The Censoring of Project #17: Hypertext Bodies and Censorship." <u>Kairos</u> 2.2 (Fall 1997): 14 secs. 6 Mar. 1998 <http://english.ttu.edu/kairos/2.2/index_f.html>.

Article in a Magazine
Viagas, Robert, and David Lefkowitz. "<u>Capeman</u> Closing Mar. 28." <u>Playbill</u> 5 Mar. 1998. 6 Mar. 1998 <http://www1.playbill.com/cgi-bin/plb/news?cmd=show&code=30763>.

Posting to a Discussion List
Grumman, Bob. "Shakespeare's Literacy." Online posting. 6 Mar. 1998. Deja News. <humanities.lit.author>.

Scholarly Project
<u>Voice of the Shuttle: Web Page for Humanities Research</u>. Ed. Alan Liu. Mar. 1998. U of California Santa Barbara. 8 Mar. 1998 <http://humanitas.ucsb.edu/>.

Professional Site
<u>The Nobel Foundation Official Website</u>. The Nobel Foundation. 28 Feb. 1998 <http://www.nobel.se/>.

Personal Site
Thiroux, Emily. Home page. 7 Mar. 1998 <http://academic.csubak.edu/home/acadpro/departments/english/engthrx.htmlx>.

Synchronous Communications (such as MOOs, MUDs, and IRCs)

Ghostly Presence. Group Discussion. telnet 16 Mar. 1997
    <moo.du.org:8000/80anon/anonview/1 4036#focus>.

Gopher Sites

Banks, Vickie, and Joe Byers. "EDTECH." 18 Mar. 1997
    <gopher://ericyr.syr.edu:70/00/Listservs/EDTECH/README>.

FTP (File Transfer Protocol) Sites

U.S. Supreme Court directory. 6 Mar. 1998 <ftp://ftp.cwru.edu/
    U.S.Supreme.Court/>.

American Psychological Association (APA) Style Guidelines

The most recent (4th) edition of the *Publication Manual of the American Psychological Association* includes general guidelines for citing electronic sources, and the APA has published specific examples for documenting Web sources on its Web page. Go to:

http://www.apa.org/journals/webref.html

In general, document these source as you do traditional sources, giving credit to the author and including the title and date of publication. Include as much information as possible to help your reader to be able to retrieve the information. Any sources that are not generally available to your readers should be documented within the body of your writing as a personal communication but not included in your reference list. Such sources include material from listservs, newsgroups, Internet relay chats (IRCs), MOOs, MUDs, and e-mail.

According to information at the Web site for the American Psychological Association entitled "How to Cite Information From the World Wide Web"*

> All references begin with the same information that would be provided for a printed source (or as much of that information as possible). The Web information is then placed at the end of the reference. It is important to use the "Retrieved from" and the date because documents on the Web may change in content, move, or be removed from a site altogether. . . . To cite a Web site in text (but not a specific document), it's sufficient to give the address (e.g., http://www.apa.org) there. No reference entry is needed.
>
> *http://www.apa.org/journals/webref.html

Use the following guidelines to include a source in your reference list:

Name of author [if given]. (Publication date) [in parentheses]. Title of the article [following APA guidelines for capitalization]. Title of periodical or electronic text [underlined]. Volume number and/or pages [if any]. Retrieved [include the date here] from the World Wide Web: [include the URL here, and do not end with a period]

Examples:
Journal Article

Fine, M. A. & Kurdek, L. A. (1993, November). Reflections on determining authorship credit and authorship order on faculty-student collaborations. <u>American Psychologist, 48.11,</u> 1141-1147. Retrieved March 6, 1998 from the World Wide Web: http://www.apa.org/journals/amp/kurdek.html

Newspaper Article

Murray, B. (1998, February). Email bonding with your students. <u>APA Monitor</u> [Newspaper, selected stories on line]. Retrieved March 6, 1998 from the World Wide Web: http://www.apa.org/monitor/bond.html

Glossary
Fasten Your Seatbelts
Jargon to Go

And a technological extension of our bodies designed to alleviate physical stress can bring on psychic stress that may be much worse.

ActiveX This is a resource developed by Microsoft to extend the function of their *Internet Explorer* software.

Archie This is a search tool used to find resources that are stored on Internet-based FTP servers. Archie is short for Archive because it performs an archive search for resources. (See *FTP* and *Server*.)

AVI This stands for Audio/Video Interleaved. It is a Microsoft Corporation format for encoding video and audio for digital transmission.

Background This refers to an image or color that is present in the background of a viewed Web document. Complex images are becoming very popular as backgrounds but require a great deal more time to download. The color of the default background can be set for most Web browsers.

Bookmark This refers to a list of URLs saved within a browser. The user can edit and modify the bookmark list to add and delete URLs as the user's interests change. *Bookmark* is a term used by Netscape to refer to the user's list of URLs; *Hotlist* is used in *Mosaic* for the same purpose. (See *Hotlist, Mosaic,* and *URL*.)

Browser   This is a software program that is used to view and browse information on the Internet. Browsers are also referred to as clients. (See *Client*.)

Bulletin Board Service   This is an electronic bulletin board. It is sometimes referred to as a BBS. Information on a BBS is posted to a computer where people can access, read, and comment on it. A BBS may or may not be connected to the Internet. Some are accessible by modem dial-in only.

Cache   This refers to a section of memory that is set aside to store information that is frequently used by the computer . Most browsers will create a cache for commonly accessed images. An example might be the images appearing in the user's homepage. Retrieving images from the cache is much quicker than downloading the images from the original source each time they are required.

Chat room   This is a site that allows real-time, person-to-person interactions.

Clickable image (Clickable map)   This refers to an interface used in Web documents that allow the user to click, or select, different areas of an image and receive different responses. Clickable images are becoming a popular way to offer a user many different selections within a common visual format.

Client   This is a software program used to view information from remote computers. Clients function in a Client-Server information exchange model. This term may also be loosely applied to the computer that is used to request information from the server. (See *Server*.)

Compressed file   This refers to a file or document that has been compacted to save memory space so that it can be easily and quickly transferred through the Internet.

Download   This is the process of transferring a file, document, or program from a remote computer to a local computer. (See *Upload*.)

E-mail   This is the short name for electronic mail. E-mail is sent electronically from one person to one or many other people. Some companies have e-mail systems that are not part of the Internet.

FAQ This stands for Frequently Asked Questions. A FAQ is a file or document in which a moderator or administrator will post commonly asked questions and their answers. If you have a question, you should check for the answer in a FAQ first.

Forms This refers to an interface element used within Web documents to allow the user to send information back to a Web server. With a forms interface, the user is requested to type responses within entry windows to be returned to the server for processing. Forms rely on a server computer to process the submittals. They are becoming more common as browser and server software improve.

FTP This stands for *File Transfer Protocol*. It is a procedure used to transfer large files and programs from one computer to another. Access to the computer to transfer files may or may not require a password. Some FTP servers are set up to allow public access by anonymous log-on. This process is referred to as *Anonymous FTP*.

GIF This stands for Graphics Interchange Format. It is a format created by CompuServe to allow electronic transfer of digital images. GIF files are a commonly-used format and can be viewed by both *Macintosh* and *Windows* users.

Gopher This is a format structure and resource for providing information on the Internet. It was created at the University of Minnesota

GUI This is an acronym for Graphical User Interface. It is a combination of the appearance and the method of interacting with a computer. A GUI requires the use of a mouse to select commands on an icon-based monitor. *Macintosh* and *Windows* operating systems use GUIs.

Helper This is software that is used to help a browser view information formats that it couldn't normally view.

Homepage This refers to a Web document that a browser loads as a point of departure to browse the Internet. It also refers to a Web page maintained by an individual. In the most general sense, it is used to refer to any Web document.

Hotlist   This is a list of URLs saved within the *Mosaic* Web browser. This same list is referred to as a *Bookmark* within the Netscape Web browser.

HTML   An abbreviation for HyperText Markup Language, the common language used to write documents that appear on the World Wide Web.

HTTP   An abbreviation for HyperText Transport Protocol, the common protocol used to communicate between World Wide Web servers.

Hypertext   This refers to text elements within a document that have an embedded connection to another item. Web documents use hypertext links to access documents, images, sounds, and video files from the Internet.

Inline image   This refers to images that are viewed along with text on Web documents. All inline images are in the GIF format. JPEG format is the other common image format for Web documents; an external viewer is typically required to view JPEG documents.

Java   This is an object-oriented programming language developed by Sun Microsystems.

JavaScript   This is a scripting language developed by Netscape in cooperation with Sun Microsystems to add functionality to the basic Web page. It is not as powerful as *Java* and works primarily from the client side.

JPEG   This stands for Joint Photographic Experts Group. It is also commonly used to refer to a format used to transfer digital images. (See *Inline image*.)

Jughead   This is a service for performing searches on the Internet. (See *Archie* and *VERONICA*.)

Mosaic   This is the name of the browser that was created at the National Center for Supercomputing Applications. It was the first Web browser to have a consistent interface for the Macintosh, Windows, and UNIX environments. The success of this browser is responsible for the expansion of the Web.

MPEG This stands for Motion Picture Experts Group. It is also a format used to make, view, and transfer both digital audio and digital video files.

Newsgroup This is the name for the discussion groups that can be on the *Usenet*. Not all newsgroups are accessible through the Internet. Some are accessible only through a modem connection. (See *Usenet*.)

Plug-in This is a resource that is added to the Netscape *Navigator* to extend its basic function.

QuickTime This is a format used by Apple Computer to make, view, edit, and send digital audio and video.

Server This is a software program used to provide or serve information to remote computers. Servers function in a Client-Server information exchange model. This term may also be loosely applied to the computer that is used to serve the information. (See *Client*.)

Table This refers to a specific formatting element found in HTML pages. Tables are used on HTML documents to visually organize information.

Telnet This is the process of remotely connecting and using a computer at a distant location.

Upload This is the process of moving or transferring a document, file, or program from one computer to another computer.

URL This is an abbreviation for Universal Resource Locator. It is an address used by people on the Internet to locate documents. URLs specify the protocol for information transfer, the host computer address, the path to the desired file, and the name of the file requested.

Usenet This is a world-wide system of discussion groups, also called newsgroups. There are many thousands of newsgroups, but only a percentage of these are accessible from the Internet.

VERONICA   This stands for *Very Easy Rodent-Oriented Netwide Index to Computerized Archives*. This is a database of menu names from a large number of Gopher servers. It is a quick and easy way to search Gopher resources for information by keyword. It was developed at the University of Nevada.

VRML   This stands for Virtual Reality Markup Language. It was developed to allow the creation of virtual reality worlds. Your browser may need a specific plug-in to view VRML pages.

WAIS   This stands for Wide Area Information Servers. This is a software package that allows the searching of large indices of information on the Internet.

WAV   This stands for Waveform sound format. It is a Microsoft Corporation format for encoding sound files.

Web (WWW)   This stands for the World Wide Web. When loosely applied, this term refers to the Internet and all of its associated elements, including Gopher, FTP, HTTP, and others. More specifically, this term refers to a subset of the servers on the Internet that use HTTP to transfer hyperlinked document in a page-like format.

Study Smarter, Not Harder.

For students taking any American government course

GOVERNMENT BY THE PEOPLE, INTERACTIVE EDITION CD-ROM
ISBN: 0-13-906603-9

- An interactive study guide offering a fundamental exploration of the political system
- 450+ photos, charts, and graphs with captions
- 120+ minutes of self-playing multimedia presentations corresponding to the chapters of the text GOVERNMENT BY THE PEOPLE, 17TH EDITION
- Hybrid CD-ROM for Macintosh® or Microsoft® Windows.

MULTIMEDIA GUIDE TO AMERICAN GOVERNMENT CD-ROM
ISBN: 0-13-340456-0

- A generic American government CD-ROM which can be used as a study guide
- A video library, data library, chart library, and political dictionary
- Interesting American government simulations
- Compatible with Microsoft® Windows.

THE POLITICAL SCIENCE STUDENT WRITER'S MANUAL
Gregory M. Scott and Stephen M. Garrison,
ISBN: 0-13-620800-4

Designed to help you write well in your Political Science class and beyond.

Pick up any of these Prentice Hall products in your bookstore, or order by calling 1-800-947-7700 using the ISBN numbers listed.